Teaching
for a
Living
Democracy

Teaching for a Living Democracy

PROJECT-BASED LEARNING IN THE ENGLISH AND HISTORY CLASSROOM

JOSHUA BLOCK

Foreword by Carla Shalaby

TEACHERS COLLEGE PRESS

TEACHERS COLLEGE | COLUMBIA UNIVERSITY

NEW YORK AND LONDON

Published by Teachers College Press,® 1234 Amsterdam Avenue, New York, NY 10027

Library of Congress Cataloging-in-Publication Data

Names: Block, Joshua, author.
Title: Teaching for a living democracy : project-based learning in the
    English and history classroom / Joshua Block.
Description: New York : Teachers College Press, 2020. | Includes
    bibliographical references and index.
Identifiers: LCCN 2020001499 (print) | LCCN 2020001500 (ebook) | ISBN
    9780807764169 (paperback) | ISBN 9780807764176 (hardback) | ISBN
    9780807778708 (ebook)
Subjects: LCSH: Project method in teaching. | Activity programs in
    education. | English language--Study and teaching (Secondary) |
    History--Study and teaching (Secondary) | Democracy and education. |
    Education, Urban.
Classification: LCC LB1027.43 .B56 2020 (print) | LCC LB1027.43 (ebook) |
    DDC 371.3/6--dc23
LC record available at https://lccn.loc.gov/2020001499
LC ebook record available at https://lccn.loc.gov/2020001500

ISBN 978-0-8077-6416-9 (paper)
ISBN 978-0-8077-6417-6 (hardcover)
ISBN 978-0-8077-7870-8 (ebook)

Printed on acid-free paper
Manufactured in the United States of America

For Jessi, Hanna, and Nati.
In many ways, you are my teachers.

Contents

Foreword

Indeed, it is precisely in a period of great spiritual and societal hunger like our own that we most need to open minds, hearts, and memories to those times when women and men¹ actually dreamed of new possibilities for our nation, for our world, and for their own lives. It is now that we may be able to convey the stunning idea that dreams, imagination, vision, and hope are actually powerful mechanisms in the creation of new realities—especially when the dreams go beyond speeches and songs to become embodied—to take on flesh, in real, hard places.

Vincent Harding (2007), *Is America Possible?*

Because I dream of education as a site for the teaching of love and the learning of liberation, I want teachers to understand themselves as powerful, necessary actors in the historic and ongoing struggle for freedom. I imagine the classroom as one "real, hard place" in which we might embody our dreams of the America we want, need, and know is possible—a place to imagine that America and to practice that America together with young people—developing the skills, dispositions, and knowledge required to steadfastly and strategically demand that America.

In my dreams at the intersection of education and organizing, I am searching—always—for ideas about and examples of daily classroom work that can support us in "creating new realities" rather than training ourselves and our young people to replicate, sustain, and better tolerate current and rampant dehumanizing, demoralizing realities. In my search, I am delighted to find Joshua Block's book—his invitation to us to teach for the creation of a new reality, to teach for what he calls "a living democracy."

Simultaneously inspirational and useful, this book is a visionary, hopeful invitation to dream and a practical, generous resource for translating our dreams into concrete new realities of teaching and learning. What a rare combination in a single text, and a gift that only a practicing teacher working and speaking from direct, daily experience is positioned to offer. We need books like this, written by teachers for teachers that offer practical guidance without disrespecting our profession with scripted how-to steps, while attempting to translate dreams to reality with just the right balance of authority and humility, and recognizing the tension that justice educators will always navigate between the constraints of schooling and the liberating possibilities of education. Joshua's energy jumps off these pages, reinvigorating my own at a soul-weary time. He reveals to us his efforts in working with young people in ways that recognize and leverage their power to lead the America we know is possible; we witness how he works to navigate the inevitable and thorny challenges that emerge. His living democracy is not free of conflict, tension, or constraint. What democracy could be?

Readers of this book do not need to abandon all naysaying tendencies—our natural desire to approach possibility with cynicism, to couple hope with skepticism—that name all the ways our constraints are more constraining than Joshua's, all the ways his possibilities aren't possible for us. But by way of preparing readers to get the most out of this book, I do invite us to momentarily do our best to resurrect our capacity for the kind of "imagination, vision, and hope" that Vincent Harding reminds us are required for the creation of new realities. Joshua's humility will support you in that effort, as this is a book that never says, "Do it this way; it's perfect," but instead says, "Here's what I tried. What do you think you might try?"

Accept this invitation to try. Joshua is insisting on different, more human purposes for schooling than the ones we have now, and he is repositioning teachers and young people to better meet those purposes by reminding them of their power and translating that reminder into concrete classroom practice. I am grateful to add this book to my own collection, and will eagerly pull it off my shelf every time a teacher asks what teaching for love and learning for freedom might look like in the daily life of a classroom. I will return to this book when I become so overwhelmed by the current realities that I cannot muster the energy to retrieve my dreams of a new reality. I will recommend it to all those ready to imagine and to enact education as a site of liberation, to those who revere the power of young people enough to create classrooms as spaces to leverage their brilliance and creativity toward making America possible.

Carla Shalaby

NOTE

1. While wishing to maintain the integrity of the original quote, I also want to recognize and be sure to include the community of non-binary and gender-nonconforming people who may not see themselves in phrases like "women and men." These individuals are a crucial part of our movement to answer the question of whether America is possible.

REFERENCE

Harding, V. (2018). *Is America possible? A letter to my young companions on the journey of hope.* Kalamazoo, MI: Fetzer Institute. Retrieved from fetzer.org/sites/default/files/images/resources/attachment/2018-03-16/FI_DAD_Harding_E-Version-Rev_0.pdf

Acknowledgments

I am held up by many and owe debts of gratitude for the support I received writing this book and building a teaching life. To the hundreds of young people who challenged me and uplifted me, helping me discover what it can truly mean to teach and be in community, I thank you. Thanks to my colleagues past and present for conversations, support, and insights. It is a blessing to be surrounded by so many reflective, critical educators. In particular, I am grateful for my close comrades and frequent collaborators Michael Clapper, Melanie Manuel, Tim Best, Amal Giknis, and others. Thank you to Chris Lehmann for school leadership that allows others to flourish and for your tireless efforts on behalf of students and teachers.

Susan Lytle, you were the midwife for this project. You provided the initial nudge and remained by my side, offering love and critique as you pushed my thinking and writing forward. This would not be the work it is without you. Thank you to Kira Baker-Doyle for mentorship and advice throughout the process. Thank you to Melanie Manuel, Matt Guynn, and John Taylor-Baranik for responding to drafts, supporting me to improve the work. Thank you Ann Farnsworth-Alvear for using your credentials to supply me with a steady stream of books and access to resources.

My time in Aotearoa, New Zealand was a gift, expanding my understandings of learning and culture. Fulbright New Zealand hosted me, Azra Moeed provided mentorship and hospitality, Michael Harcourt shared insights and offered support, and Ann Milne responded with wonderful critique of this work.

I am grateful for the insights and vision of my editor, Emily Spangler, and have deep appreciation for the ways she thoughtfully supported me throughout this process. Thanks to the multiple people at TC Press who skillfully helped bring this book into the world. Carla Shalaby, thank you for so generously writing such a beautiful foreword. Carla's work strongly impacted me and my stance as a teacher/author. Readers, if you haven't yet read *Troublemakers*, make it your next book!

My ancestors came to this land in search of new lives. Their journeys and experiences as foreigners allowed me to grow up with privileges and comforts they could not have imagined. Thank you to my parents, Paul Block and Ellen Stone, for the different ways they supported me to become what I hope is a version of my ancestors' dreams.

Finally, Jessi, your love, your knowing heart, and our shared lives ground me in this world. Hanna and Nati, thank you for your insights, feistiness, and compassion. You all are so much of who I am.

CHAPTER 1

Reframing School Learning

We need an expanded vocabulary, adequate to both the daily joy and the daily sorrow of our public schools. And we are in desperate need of rich, detailed images of possibility.

—Mike Rose (2009)

In the hallway students occupied a section of the not-so-clean floor. They lay sprawled on their stomachs, facing three laptops, legs angled in different directions. "We've got a really good idea," Liza offered as she saw me approaching. "We want to teach them about Columbus Day."

"Can that work?" asked Jules. "They've probably never *really* thought about it before."

Outside the classroom and in the room at tables, on the floor, and in a clump near the windowsill, student groups from a 12th-grade English class were huddled together, some eagerly sharing ideas and some tentatively investigating possibilities as they planned lessons to teach to a 6th-grade class at a nearby elementary school. The 12th-graders had spent several weeks interrogating different meanings, understandings, and experiences of literacy. They had heard the 6th-grade teacher's description of his students and topics that class had been studying. Now they were tasked with designing literacy-based lessons for this group of younger students. The stakes felt high. I had made it clear that no one would be approved to teach until their group showed me a completed, thoughtfully developed lesson plan based on the template I gave them (see Appendix, section B).

The scene reflected different experiences of young people engaged in real-world work. Some groups were actively researching and planning, working together to develop ideas they all agreed upon. They could be heard proposing plans, continually reassessing ideas, and searching for resources. Other groups were devising lessons that didn't yet meet criteria for the assignment or for success at the elementary school. Still others were having a hard time identifying and agreeing on lesson goals and needed the facilitation and encouragement of a teacher to nudge them forward.

Underneath the chaos was the undeniable power of young people engaging in work that has meaning. There was no talk about grades and little avoidance of the work. Instead, groups were remembering what they were like as 6th graders as they strategized different ways to engage 11-year-olds. Liza's group, focusing on cultural literacy, had discovered a video that asked the viewers to reconsider Columbus Day and were debating different ways to ask 6th-graders to reflect on the holiday and to consider the alternative celebration of Indigenous People's Day. Audrey, Aaron, and Donesha were deciding how to use their lesson to raise the idea of gender as a social construct. The classroom and the hallway were filled with a chorus of student voices alternating among discovery, debate, frustration, and excitement.

The background for this moment was the work I had done to prepare students to design lessons and work independently on projects for public audiences. Students knew that the work of the class prioritized their ideas and that the responsibility of developing quality products fell on them. They also knew that I was available to offer support and that we shared a vision of successful lessons and engaged intellectual experiences.

Earlier in the week I had modeled a lesson for the class based on the planning framework they were using. We analyzed the lesson and my design choices together. I made my thinking about my own planning process clear to them, so they could understand how I translate objectives and content into a lesson format. Then the class generated a list of goals and things to avoid for the project. Students also had a list of potential lesson topics, initially generated by me and supplemented with ideas brainstormed by the class. In addition, students had access to a collection of resource links I had compiled and shared.

I continually checked in with different groups and nudged them forward in the process. Even when students didn't realize I was listening, I was tuned in to what was happening within the groups, observing interpersonal dynamics and paying attention to the content they were developing. Prepared with a framework, careful prompting, and opportunities to collaborate, the students did the intellectual work of transforming their ideas into a purposeful sequence of activities for 6th-graders.

TEACHING FOR A LIVING DEMOCRACY

This book is about ways teachers can change the experience of school for students. It is about different pathways for developing transgressive, or boundary-crossing, teaching practices that continue to grow with time. In her seminal book on the topic, bell hooks describes student feelings of recognition, communal experience, and the ability to "re-inscribe systems of domination" as core elements of transgressive education (hooks, 2017, pp. 8–10). Correspondingly, the pedagogies and practices within this book are based on the idea that *relationships* are at the root of all good teaching and learning, providing a foundation that enables students to invest themselves in work that aims to rewrite the world. Seeing education as experiences of connection and expression allows us to understand the ways education can change students' and teachers' understandings of themselves and their roles in society. These new intelligences lead to transformation and different ways of living. A daily reality that is engaged and critically reflective leads to democratic actions and behaviors that change lives and help remake societies (Dewey, 1933). In this vision of education, classrooms are communities grappling with issues and conflicts while creating products and ideas. These pedagogies are an extension of Grace Lee Boggs's belief that "Children need to be given a sense of the 'unique capacity of human beings to shape and create reality in accordance with conscious purposes and plans'" (Boggs & Kurashige, 2012, p. 90).

My goal is to encourage innovative, local pedagogy, which is to say learning experiences that engage and challenge students based on who they are and current issues within their society and community. This book provides a framework to assist teachers in designing curriculum of their own, creating opportunities for students to produce work relevant to their lived realities. This type of teaching creates scenarios in which school learning matters deeply to students. These authentic learning experiences can be difficult to quantify. While the learning easily meets, and typically exceeds, standards and outside requirements, the end results cannot be accurately judged with a test score or checklist. Yet any observer can bear witness to students' deep intellectual exploration and the life-affirming qualities of growth and collaboration.

When school encourages intellectual exploration and innovation, students reconfigure understandings of themselves, their capabilities, and their roles in the world. In this context student creations are manifestations of a living democracy, meaning student work and thought continually develop new social and individual narratives through deep analysis, critical reflection, and creative expression for wider audiences. These acts can be understood as daily or living democratic behaviors and habits that speak back to regressive forces within society and speak toward the society we choose to help build. It is a form of civics education that extends beyond a class on government and rejects the belief that the public role of citizens in a democracy is limited to voting. These ways of teaching and learning challenge authoritarian trends and the pressure to silently conform to unjust systems.

Rather than viewing democracy as a theoretical concept, classrooms and schools that operate in these ways embrace Saul Alinsky's ideas of a dynamic democracy, "a vibrant, living sweep of hope and progress which constantly strives for its objective in life, the search for truth, justice, and the dignity of [wo]man" (Baldwin, Hercules, & Orenstein, 1999). Teaching with a vision of these democratic ideals changes the purpose and understandings of the daily reality of school.

Teaching for a living democracy means utilizing classroom practices and curriculum that result in students developing a stance of self-awareness, critical thought, participation, and social agency. In this model of learning, students develop larger understandings of voice and their own abilities. To frame what happens with my students as a practice of living democracy may seem to be overly idealistic or even arrogant. I do not propose this connection lightly but hold it up as an intention and an aspiration.

Teaching in this way requires a paradigm shift where, instead of viewing students as deficient or lacking knowledge (Freire, 2005), we understand young people as having rich, varied life experiences, creativity, and capability, all of which are utilized to develop original ideas and produce work that has meaning beyond the walls of a classroom. Thinking of education and the work of schools in this way means assuming a stance of, and belief in, creativity and potential. Instead of accepting school as a system of uniformity (Illich, 1983), teachers can work to make school a place that helps students develop what Hannah Arendt described as "sphere[s] of freedom" (Arendt, 2018, p. 30). These experiences are what Maxine Greene calls "more vibrant ways of being in the world" (Greene, 2000, p. 5).

This book is based on the premise that teaching for a living democracy is a complex, constantly evolving practice that should be understood as a process of individual and collective engagement and transformation for both students and teachers. There is a rich history of theory describing these types of teaching and learning developed by progressive educators during different time periods. In "My Pedagogic Creed," John Dewey wrote that education must be "a process of living and not a preparation for future living" (Dewey, 1897, p. 78). In other words, the experience of school should have meaning in the present. An abstract notion of preparation for the future is not meaningful for students and does not sustain interest nor engagement. More than half a century after Dewey, Paolo Freire envisioned education as a practice of freedom, and a way to enact change in the world. He wrote of the need to allow learners "to be more fully human . . . in the authentic struggle to change the situation [of oppression]" (Freire, 2005, p. 47). Maxine Greene raised the idea that individuals must experience a creative, solution-oriented process within their work and that education must be more than a limited practice: "People trying to be more fully human must not only engage in critical thinking but must be able to imagine something coming of their hopes; their silence must be overcome by their search" (Greene, 2000, p. 25). This is a participatory, continually evolving pedagogy that emphasizes experimentation and creativity (the search) rather than passivity (silence).

This kind of teaching requires a mindset in which educators undertake what Shanti Elliott describes as rethinking "the frame of the adult–child hierarchy," and practicing "a trust in human capacity" (Elliott, 2015, pp. 4 and 8). These pedagogies are student-centered and involve a strategic balance of intellectual leadership, relationship building, mentorship, and consultation. The result is that students are able to explore the margins of identities and society (Greene, 2000, p. 28). Teaching for a living democracy means creating opportunities for communities of students to explore texts and ideas deeply, to produce work that expresses insights and new understandings in imaginative ways, and to share their work among appreciative peers and wider audiences.

The values and insights of these progressive theorists, whom I consider my education forebears and companions, are deeply embedded within the book. This work would not be possible without the path that they cleared. In addition, this work is sustained and carried forward by the insights of contemporary teachers and teaching networks that regularly develop and share resources and ideas designed to change the experience and meaning of school for students. It is a privilege to know so many talented educators and to have access to a wealth of resources, online and off. It is impossible for me to imagine a teaching career without the inspiration and knowledge of others, which I benefit from on a regular basis.

Ultimately this book is meant to challenge the idea that students of any background should be subject to simplistic or rote learning experiences that limit their opportunities for growth while diminishing their humanity. It is my goal to provide a dynamic framework to help educators envision and construct pedagogies and practices that bring these ideas to fruition in classrooms and other educational spheres.

CHANGING THE GRAMMAR OF SCHOOLING

Much of what informs our thinking about learning and school is unconscious. Within the revolutionary promise of a public education system, the structure of many schools evolved in ways that minimized creative potential for students (Illich, 1983). Most of us were brought up attending institutions that were modeled after schools built on beliefs of conformity and shallow ideas of education. This inherited "grammar of schooling" has left us with a remarkable dearth of models in which teachers facilitate the joyful, creative, empowering potential inherent in meaningful learning (Tyack & Cuban, 1995).

Teaching in this way requires us to transgress dominant ideas of schooling. By challenging these often unspoken yet widely accepted understandings of school, we are able to transform unremarkable class periods into experiences of engagement and meaning. In this model teachers frame learning as inquiry and take on the roles of guides and intellectual leaders, assisting students as they produce work that reflects their interests and passions, pointing students toward new resources, questions, models, and often, to each other as helpers and sources.

The strategies in this book are designed to help teachers resist thin, mechanistic visions of teaching and learning. By avoiding practices that diminish the potential and joy of teaching and learning, teachers develop a sustainable, life-affirming practice. My experience is that learning is deeper when student voices are nurtured and supported as young people investigate, collaborate, and develop original ideas. Rejecting the view that students are deficient or lacking knowledge or that teachers have a monopoly on knowledge and need to *deliver* content, teachers can see young people as having rich, varied life experiences, creativity, and capability, all of which are utilized to develop original questions and ideas and to produce work that has meaning and impact beyond the walls of a classroom.

In order to change the grammar of school, we must understand the experience of school for students, with a special focus on the experiences of students who struggle in school. In many ways these struggling or disengaged students are the canaries in the coal mine, warning us to pay closer attention to the multiple ways schools fail to engage young people. The ideas in this book serve to transform the experience of school for all students and are particularly transformational for those students who have not been successful in traditional school settings.

MY TEACHING CONTEXT AND BACKGROUND

My understandings of schools and education are rooted in practitioner inquiry and my daily classroom practice as a high school Humanities teacher. I have been a project-based English and History teacher at urban high schools for most of the last 20 years, spending thousands of hours with young people as I seek to understand how to make school more than a compulsory experience for mixed groups of learners. I am certified and regularly teach in two disciplines, although my pedagogy and praxis emphasize the learning experiences of students over regimented ideas of content. There are times when a class is easily identified as English or History and other days when the subject can be seen as Humanities or maybe even more broadly as *inquiry and creation.*

For most of my teaching career, I have been a teacher at Science Leadership Academy (SLA), a highly regarded, inquiry- and project-based Philadelphia public magnet high school. SLA is a racially and socioeconomically diverse school with a student body drawn from every zip code in our city. This means that I teach students who arrive at school with basic needs unmet, as well as those who come from more affluent backgrounds. I teach some students for whom attending a mixed high school is the first time they are having meaningful interactions with people from outside their neighborhood, other students whose families immigrated from different parts of the world, and still others whose affluence and privilege have given them access to a wide range of experiences and opportunities. There is little common ground among our students before they come to us.

As a teacher at a Philadelphia public school, I also have the experience of working within the constraints and mandates of an underfunded urban district and a larger education bureaucracy. Our class sizes are large, facilities are in disrepair, and school budgets regularly lack funding for an appropriate number of teachers and staff. While our school embraces inquiry- and project-based learning, we also have to negotiate the requirements of state standards and administer state-mandated tests. I point this out because the teaching I write about in this book takes place in a larger climate that is often not supportive. At SLA we are able to continue to do what we do because we have strong leadership, make sure to meet necessary outside requirements, and maintain a consistent focus on meaningful learning for students.

Teaching at SLA has helped me to discover ways to support and challenge students with many different life and academic histories. At SLA we work to collaboratively practice an "ethic of care" (Noddings, 2002), and share the philosophy that technology should be widely available and strategically integrated into learning (Lehmann & Chase, 2015). To these ends we fundraise in order to have a one-to-one laptop program and we encourage students to use their devices to implement the school's core values of inquiry, research, collaboration, presentation, and reflection. Students final projects are often posted on public blogs, and students are regularly asked to present their work to wider audiences. My students accompany me to academic conferences, they share their work with artists and experts, and I promote and publicize their work through social media and blog posts.

One goal in providing an overview of my school is to emphasize that the ideas and pedagogies in this book can be implemented for a wide range of learners in multiple contexts. It is a falsehood that progressive learning practices only work for some kids. Many of my most fulfilling teaching memories are of students who, for one reason or another, had not had positive experiences in school but who now created work that allowed them to discover their academic abilities and new aspects of themselves. Other students I have worked with have a history of doing well in school but find that their connection to the work of school transforms when they are asked to create work that has greater meaning. Ultimately, this book is built upon my belief in equity and an understanding that we need to change what quality public education means in our democracy.

AGENCY AND POSSIBILITY

Teaching should be a deeply creative and intellectual practice. In order for teachers to make school a place of meaning they must be immersed in content; they must be tuned in to and responsive to individual students and the inner life of groups (Lakey, 2010); and they must be able to assess and quickly adapt to classroom events and dynamics. Teaching in this way makes classrooms places where students see themselves as agents, not subjects. Learning becomes an exercise of imagination and possibility rather than an exercise in conformity and compliance.

The ways teachers structure learning experiences is one of the most important factors in determining learners' understandings of content and of themselves. Meaningful experiences are not the product of teachers sharing information they have acquired. Instead, school and learning matter most when students are engaged in processes of inquiry and discovery. Deep learning happens when students are engaged in what can be messy, unpredictable processes of co-creating work that is intellectually stimulating and has meaning beyond the walls of school.

These types of teaching and learning require changes in classroom norms. Instead of a self-contained space, class becomes a place for communication with outside experts and for exploring connections between students' lived realities and course content. Class time is devoted to collaboration, student design and decisionmaking, and critical feedback for the work of peers, not to competition. These practices require teachers to intentionally create stimulating, nurturing, intellectual community.

This book offers a framework for learning design and should not be read as a manual. The framework is based on the premise that the best pedagogy is local, creative, and relevant to students. When school is an experience of co-creation, students are challenged to redefine and enrich their understandings of self and the world. In order to illustrate this, student voices, classroom moments, and student-created work saturate the text. The voices of youth are positioned in the foreground to show the spontaneity and struggle embedded in the daily reality of a classroom. It is through the thoughts, experiences, and creations of young people that we are best able to envision what education can be and what a living democracy can mean.

One reason that many people in education do not focus on pedagogical innovation is that they are continually forced to fight for educational equity. Because the education conditions that exist in wealthy and poor areas of our country are so different (Kozol, 2005), many educators must focus their efforts on the struggle for resources or on the necessary work of claiming the promise of equitable public education for all. Yet, at the same time, we need to work toward a model that inspires and transforms, not merely a model that replicates limited ideas of schooling. My own educational experiences inside and outside of school and my experiences as a teacher taught me that it is possible to make schools, and classrooms, places of passion, engagement, and meaning. Equity is about resources but it is also about changing the student experience of school, thus changing the society we live in.

The good news is that more and more teachers, administrators, policymakers, and members of the public are beginning to question the value of old, deficient models of learning and school. School learning can be an experience that affirms the humanity of students and teachers. Classrooms can be places of risk and affirmation where young intellectuals grapple with deep questions and creative beings produce projects that speak to consequential issues in the world. Yet it is not until we acknowledge the complexity, the messiness, and a richer meaning of learning that we will be able to design classrooms and schools that regularly transgress the dominant model.

The pages that follow offer narratives of classroom practices and processes for planning inquiry- and project-based units that lead to learning experiences where students *create* knowledge. Chapter 2 offers an account of several different units of study and focuses on the idea of designing curriculum for deep learning. Chapter 3 focuses on elevating student voices and truths, exploring different ways the lives and experiences of students can be centered alongside a process of academic inquiry. Chapter 4 investigates ways teachers can change the dynamics of classroom learning by inhabiting multiple roles to support student growth. Chapter 5 integrates insights I gained from visiting New Zealand schools and investigates ways to decolonize school. Chapter 6 takes a closer look at moments of classroom discomfort and friction in the context of teaching for a living democracy.

I believe that school can be a place of meaning, experimentation, and creation. My work with students regularly reminds me that learning matters when it allows people to take risks while they reconstruct and reexamine themselves, their roles, and the potential for their voices in the world. I hope that this book demonstrates different ways that supporting students to discover passion through real-world work can nurture and enrich both students and teachers.

CHAPTER 2

Designing Curriculum
for Deeper Learning

[A]ll children could and should be inventors of their own theories, critics
of other people's ideas, analyzers of evidence, and makers of their own
personal marks on this most complex world. It's an idea with revolutionary implications. If we take it seriously.

—Deborah Meier, 2005

When I am in the midst of designing new units of study for my students
it is impossible to deny the deeply intellectual, creative, joyful mess that
is a teaching life. My research and quest for inspiration do not cease.
When I see an exhibit, read a poem, hear a radio piece, or just speak
with friends, my mind is in curriculum mode. How can young people do
a version of this work? Can my students create products to complement
or speak back to others' narratives? Is there an opportunity for collaboration and for my students to have learning experiences beyond the
walls of school?

This chapter is about the process of planning units that embody the
ideas of a living democracy. My goal is to debunk the myth of the necessity of educational conformity and standardization that has dominated
recent discourse around schools in the United States (Hagopian, 2015;
Ravitch, 2011). I will share pathways that allowed me to create innovative, local pedagogies to elevate student voices and provide opportunities for students to transform themselves and their understandings. Like
the rest of this book, this chapter does not prescribe specific formulas
or tricks but sets forth a framework meant to be adapted and individu-
alized. The examples articulate the range of considerations and design
choices that go into planning units that lead to deeper learning.

IMMIGRATION ORAL HISTORY PROJECTS

While some of my students have immigration stories of their own or are growing up in households where they hear relatives' or parents' immigration stories, many others know little about the experiences of immigrants. As debates raged about Dreamers (people who came to the United States at young ages and have undocumented status) and anti-immigrant rhetoric became more public, I set myself to designing curriculum that would speak to issues and experiences relating to immigration within the United States. The initial motivation for designing this unit was based in knowledge about my students' lives and a desire to validate experiences of some while expanding understanding of contemporary issues—often misrepresented and misunderstood—in ways that would be meaningful to all.

Knowing that this unit would include large amounts of different types of reading, writing, and oral communication, I did not preoccupy myself with ELA standards; these would be easy to identify and document later in my planning process. Because the work my students produce is sophisticated and complex, their learning always incorporates multiple skills that correlate to outside standards. I never use the criteria of national and state standards as a starting point for the development of a learning plan, instead choosing to first focus on the intellectual and creative potential within curriculum design, attempting to center meaningful goals for the learning experiences of students.

I began looking for inspiration and sources while deciding on the goals for the unit (Wiggins & McTighe, 2005):

- What essential questions would the class investigate?
- At the end of the unit, what did I want students to understand?
- What would they create that would engage them and lead them toward the goals I was developing?

A significant part of the early planning involved educating myself. I knew little about the reality of living in this country without documentation. Feeling some shame about my ignorance, I began reading articles, essays, and books; I also turned toward people I know and asked them questions. Through my research, I realized that, like many others, I had multiple false assumptions and managed to coexist with people who lived realities I had not attempted to fully understand. I was introduced to Jose Antonio Vargas's film *Documented* (2013), which sheds light on the lives of undocumented immigrants and Dreamers in our country. After watching the film, I began reading about the work of different immigrant rights organizations. I read several novels by authors from different parts of the world, looking for examples of global fiction that would help my many students who had very little international experience or understanding develop their knowledge. I was given the book *Forty-Cent Tip* (Three New York International High Schools, 2006), a collection of stories about immigrant workers compiled by high school students. I reached out to others in my network to learn more and find additional sources.

Throughout my process of self-education and discovery I focused on identifying themes that could be used to frame learning for students. Often a reference in one source would lead me to another text. As I researched I paid attention to controversy and debates, beginning the early, nonlinear stage of developing project ideas that would have meaning to the students and ideally to others beyond the walls of our classroom. The amount of information felt a bit overwhelming but, as usually happens when I plan, I was developing passion for what I was learning. I was surprised by how much I didn't know but, as I educated myself, I realized that there was information and ideas that others also needed to know. This immersion in learning was stimulating, and reminded me of the experience I wished to create for my students.

I outlined what I saw as the two strands of the unit. First, in order to develop more international awareness and deeper understanding of the conditions that push families toward immigration, students would read a work of global fiction. I identified five books by authors with different backgrounds that they could choose from. They would read and discuss with book groups. This decentralized structure and the acts of generating questions and running discussions without the help of a teacher would help students develop a level of independence with their work. In addition to their work in groups, I would create several assignments to make sure that they understood the historical context for their book and demonstrated comprehension and analysis of the texts.

The goal of the second thread of the unit was for students to develop an in-depth understanding of immigration and the different experiences of immigrants and refugees in Philadelphia. Students would develop background knowledge on and understanding of current immigration trends in the United States through nonfiction readings and interviews. It felt important to provide students with a method for processing the information they would find. One strategy I identified was to ask them to sort information into categories that either confirmed previous knowledge or challenged their assumptions or understandings. I gathered articles and developed additional questions and frameworks for these activities. I was careful to limit the number of goals for the unit overall to two; I wanted our inquiry to have a clear focus, and the two topics of the unit felt expansive and worthy of exploration without additional, potentially confusing, topics or directives.

We would watch Vargas's documentary, *Documented* (2013). I would begin by asking students whether the language we used to describe people's status (undocumented or illegal) was significant. This could be an opener to a larger discussion about perceptions of immigrants. I created a sheet for students to record key quotes as they watched the film, and then make a list of ideas revealed by the film.

At this point I began to focus on what students would create during the second half of the unit, when the learning goal was to develop in-depth understandings of different experiences of immigrants and refugees. I reminded myself that the culminating work of the unit needed to provide a rationale for the work we were doing throughout the unit. If at any point a student asked me why we were looking at a particular source or talking about a certain topic, I wanted to be able to explain the connection to the upcoming final project.

Based on their reading of different works of fiction and multiple nonfiction sources during the unit, one of the understandings that I anticipated hearing from students was that immigration means paying attention to individual stories. Through my conversations with others I had been introduced to the director of a local nonprofit, The Welcoming Center, that teaches English to recent immigrants. My communication with the head of the organization had opened a window of possibility. When I had asked about a project we could collaborate on, the staff there proposed having my students interview their clients, recent immigrants who were learning English and job skills, with the goals of developing digital profile projects that they could use for fundraising purposes and having students help clients set up professional social media accounts. It would be an opportunity for English Learners (the clients) to practice their language skills and make cultural connections. The collaboration had enormous potential but also worried me. Would my teenaged students be able to meet the requirements of a professional environment? Would they create work of a high-enough quality to do justice to the stories and the people they would be interviewing? I needed to find ways to structure the work and clarify expectations, but I also needed to let go of my anxiety and give my students a chance to show me and others their capabilities.

Three weeks into the unit, we were immersed in global fiction and different sources relating to the political and personal realities of immigration. Multiple pages of student notebooks were filled with ideas, observations, and questions. I introduced the Welcoming Center collaboration by handing out three different one-page immigration profile pieces. One came from *The New York Times Magazine* (Phunthavong, 2015) and two came from the book *Forty-Cent Tip* (Three New York International High Schools, 2006). Each of these short, first-person essays presented a personal narrative of immigration, capturing key elements of the individuals' experiences and related emotions.

> "What do you notice? Read the three pieces with your table and record a list in your journals. What different things do these pieces teach us and what can you tell about how they were created? Make sure you have at least eight bullet points when we talk in twenty minutes."

I hadn't yet given the students many details of our outside collaboration and was gambling on the fact that these models would help sell them on the value of short profile pieces that used stories to reveal the human impacts of different aspects of immigrants' experiences. I floated around the room as groups read, sometimes prodding with questions or affirming ideas or observations I heard. As we transitioned to a whole-class discussion, I was aware of the many factors at play, ready to facilitate and, if need be, steer the discussion in a direction that I hoped would be helpful.

> "All right! Can everyone turn around so you can see others? What did you find? What seems important to point out to other people? You all do the talking, I'll make a list on the board. Please add what I write to the lists you already have in your journals. Edwin, you want to start?"
>
> "I liked the way that these are written so that you feel like you are there with the person."
>
> I nodded at Kara, who was raising her hand, as I wrote. She spoke: "Yeah. These must have been interviews but you don't see the questions. You just hear the story."
>
> "Excellent points. Kara, call on someone else who has their

hand raised." I turned back to the board, ready to add to the list of student ideas I had begun recording.

The ideas continued to come. I was mainly the board scribe, although at times I stepped in with questions for clarification or asked students' permission to revise the language of their idea in order to write it on the list concisely or clearly. Occasionally, I contributed an idea of my own with the knowledge that I wanted this list to serve as a list of goals for the work that we would soon begin with The Welcoming Center.

Once we had generated a strong list of ideas, I introduced our outside collaboration and gave a brief overview of The Welcoming Center. Then we were ready to talk more about their project.

> "Right now I am sharing a doc with you that describes your project for the last part of this unit. Take a minute to get on your screens so we can look at it all together."

Once they are all logged on, I asked one student to begin reading the project description and list of tips for success to the class. I tried to keep this document concise with the knowledge that too much information at this point would lead to confusion.

Project Description

Working in a group of 2–3 people:

I. Help your Welcoming Center client create a professional LinkedIn or Facebook page, including a resume.
II. Complete at least three thirty-minute interviews with a client at The Welcoming Center. Get stories from the interviewees that can be used to write a 500-word (approximate) profile focusing on specific theme(s). Text will be accompanied by photos (can be photos of interviewee or can be symbolic photos). Give your interviewee a chance to approve and make any changes to essay and photos before publishing final website.

Tips for Success

- In interviews, the more details and stories the better
- Final product will have an intro paragraph with physical description of interviewee

- Final product will include photo montage and large block quotes to break up text
- Each profile piece should have a unique title (use a quote from interview)
- Share final draft with interviewee before publishing (they have final say on product)
- Stories should be real/raw. Don't use stats but use stories
- Capture emotion
- There should be flow in the final piece

It would be foolish to ignore the fact that once I have asked students to log on their devices, there is much more potential for distraction. When another student is reading aloud to the class, I watch people in different parts of the room going through the tell-tale motions of switching windows as they get distracted and feel compelled to check something unrelated to our course. I try to minimize this by calling on people in different parts of the room to read at different times, sometimes with warning, sometimes without. For a student who is clearly distracted I may give them a heads-up as I walk by: "I'm going to call on you to read the next paragraph."

After having heard students read multiple parts of the project description I spoke to the whole class. "Any big-picture questions that will help you understand this project before we move on to the next step? We will be going over many more specific details in the days ahead."

After answering two questions about details, I continued: "Okay. Last thing for the day—with your tablemates create a list of at least 12 questions that you think would work well as interview questions at the Welcoming Center. I need your list before class ends. Be sure to check the description of types of interview questions on the project doc."

Later that day, I used the papers I received from students to make a question bank for the class. I took questions students generated, sorted them, made small revisions when necessary, and added some of my own. The goal was to create a resource that would help all students effectively prepare for their interviews.

In the following days, we took a class trip to The Welcoming Center, meeting the staff and learning the logistics of how students would enter the office building when they began meeting with clients. I conducted a model interview of a student in front of the class, regularly pausing for feedback and observations about interview techniques. Students then conducted mock interviews with each other, practicing techniques and testing recording equipment and apps.

The following 2 weeks were a blur of activity. I set up a system for students to leave our building with permission when they had appointments at the Welcoming Center. I regularly checked our master scheduling doc where I saw different scheduled meeting times and reached out to students who didn't seem to be on track (sometimes it was just that they had not entered their information on the doc; other times a nudge was necessary.) For myself, I set up a checklist and workflow of conferences with students so that no one left for their appointments without first talking through interview strategies and showing me their own list of questions that they had selected from our question bank. I helped students regroup when a peer was absent or other obstacles emerged. At times when groups had nothing to do, I reminded them about their book groups and asked them to work on their next reading group deadline.

When the student groups returned from their interviews, I found myself peppering them with questions, eager for details. At The Welcoming Center, they were doing the work we prepped for together completely independent of me. "How did it go? I want all the details!" I joked with them, but I also felt some envy—they were making connections and learning an immense amount from the people they were working with. That said, every group's experience was different. Some groups stumbled through communication and language difficulties with clients, other groups immediately developed a close connection with the interviewee and made plans to get together outside of the school day, and others found it really hard to connect with someone who seemed reluctant to share any part of their story, despite the fact that this was an experience that clients opted in to. The groups who had successful interviews were clearly impacted by the experience.

> "I couldn't believe it. She was telling us stuff that was so crazy. She has been through so much," Candace told me when she got back to school. "We didn't really know how to respond."
>
> "What did you all say? How did you handle it?" I was concerned. Was this a situation where my students did damage or weren't able to adequately respond to a person who was telling a personal story?
>
> "We kept asking questions and we told her how amazing it was to hear her story."

The more Candace told me, the more I realized how well they had handled the situation. Even though her group was made up of three teens who were often goofy and frequently distracted in my classroom, they had been fully present, focused, and thoughtful in the real-life scenario of interviewing someone they had just met.

"Nice job. I'm really impressed with how you all did. Tomorrow at the start of class can you tell everyone about how it went?"

As the process continued, I sat with students listening to audio, I read transcripts, I processed the experience with students, and I read drafts of profile essays. While the final products represent only a partial view of what came from this process, they speak to the depth and quality of the intellectual processes and the work that were occurring. Each website has an introduction section written by students followed by a profile essay constructed from parts of the interviews. Knowing that they were creating these products for The Welcoming Center and that they would show it to the interviewee for approval meant that students pushed themselves to publish sites that were polished and graphically appealing. I worked closely with groups to help them develop introductions that went beyond obvious, blanket statements about immigration, and I pointed out areas for revision throughout the creation process. While I was the one assigning the grades, it did not feel as if I was the primary audience. This allowed me to frame my feedback as an ally who was offering ideas to improve the quality of the work rather than an instructor trying to convince students to do it my way. This helped avoid some of the power struggles that can be associated with the feedback and revision process with more traditional classroom work.

At the end of the unit, we were able to celebrate students' accomplishments. We took time to appreciate the different websites as I projected them in the front of the room and students shared final thoughts about the experience and their understandings about immigration. Some students had struggled more than others—either their interviewee didn't lend themselves to a detailed essay or logistics had proved difficult. I promised to be accommodating to details that were outside of their control in my grading and reminded students about the complicated reality of people's lives and this type of work. (See project examples in Appendix, section A.)

The unit achieved the goal of immersing students in ideas and understandings of immigration. They got beyond headlines and learned about a range of experiences and realities. Maybe most importantly, their learning was impactful because it was active and immersive. Rather than listening to me tell them all they should have learned, they had to step into the role of investigators who then had to process and contextualize their findings. Finally, they had to take these findings and present them in a larger, polished format.

Just this week I heard from someone who did this project over 4 years ago. She just graduated from college. What was the reason for her call? She remembers this project so clearly and so fondly that she wants me to re-connect her with The Welcoming Center or another organization where she can work with recent immigrants for her first full-time job after school. Her vision of meaningful work is to continue to engage with people often ignored and ostracized by mainstream society.

ADVANCED ESSAY PROCESS

One summer I was intent on developing new strategies to refresh my teaching of writing in 11th-grade English courses. I wanted to develop a trajectory that was engaging, could be developed throughout the year, and included communal elements for what can often be a very individual process. I wanted students to finish the year having written in many different styles and having developed the confidence and perseverance necessary to create insightful, polished products. I titled these papers *Advanced Essays* to help students understand I was asking for something new and wanted them to make a break from the more formulaic writing assignments many of them had become accustomed to earlier in their learning careers.

Part of my planning involved reflecting on my own writing experiences as a young person. I remember the immersive joy I felt as an elementary school student asked to write in silly and creative ways. I remember a writing conference with a professor as an undergraduate where my ideas were recognized as important. Her small offerings and insights propelled me down a clearer road of exploration and creation, helping me become more invested and excited about my work. I also remember (albeit more faintly) writing numerous assignments that meant little to me. These writing experiences seemed less about me and more about the preoccupations of the instructor or a focus on external requirements.

My negative writing experiences point to a sad truth about the way that most students learn to write: In their attempts to meet specific requirements, they become boring writers. Many students are taught to remove their own voices and detach from content, to analyze with sterile language, and to develop ideas within a narrow formula. Teachers designed structure is helpful, but if not implemented strategically, it can stifle creativity and require students to "perform" the requirements of school rather than investing themselves in creation. Attempts to help young people develop writing skills by focusing exclusively on the construction of thesis statements or a prescribed paragraph structure can actually steer students away from the joy and power of developing unique, insightful writing voices.

Peter Elbow, author of *Writing Without Teachers* (2007), adds to this analysis, emphasizing the value of a thoughtful, searching writing process:

> [T]hink of writing as an organic, developmental process in which you start writing at the very beginning—before you know your meaning at all—and encourage your words gradually to change and evolve. Only at the end will you know what you want to say or the words you want to say it with . . . Meaning is not what you start with but what you end up with. (p. 15)

With this information and my own experiences in mind, I designed a writing sequence with the goal of honoring writing as a process and pathway for discovering meaning. Instead of leading students to feel that school writing must be separate from their lived realities, I wanted my students to experience a process of creation. My hope was to encourage more students to commit themselves to the struggle of creating complex, advanced products.

Much of secondary school writing focuses on thesis-based writing. While I believe there is value to this approach, I've also come to believe that we should provide more of a range of approaches and requirements to help young people develop their writing craft. In *Occasions for Writing*, Robert DiYanni and Pat C. Hoy II offer a vision of essay writing that provides a more open structure. They frame essay writing as "mak[ing] something new, something that only you can create" (2009, p. 2), and they encourage writers to go beyond the idea of a thesis: "Rather than simply declaring a thesis in your writing—something that you intend to 'prove'—you should be actively inquiring about and developing an idea" (p. 6). This type of essay writing allows writers to use experiences and different kinds of texts as evidence that can lead to discovery. By expanding what is acceptable for an academic paper, we allow students to experiment and be creative. Because they become more engaged, they become better writers. And because they are better writers, they are better able to adapt as writing expectations shift within different contexts.

I attempt to integrate these ideas into my practice by having students write Advanced Essays at the end of inquiry-based units where we read, view, and discuss multiple texts that investigate a theme. These themes are broad and compelling, centered on topics such as Literacy; Identity and Belonging; or Violence, Militarism, and Alternatives. In each unit we begin our inquiries together as a class, reading, writing informally, discussing our ideas, and completing smaller assignments and projects. The main texts usually include a book along with a thematically linked collection of essays. When possible I will include a film, shorter videos, or other types of art that expand the inquiry and expose students to new ideas. When it comes time to begin writing the essays I provide students with a curated collection of resources beyond what we have covered together and also encourage them to research on their own as they choose a focus within the framework of the unit and develop a larger idea. (I now rarely use the words thesis and argument.) I don't have specific rules about techniques like the use of first person or the number and type of paragraphs that should be in an essay. Instead, I guide students by speaking about evidence and the development of analysis and larger ideas. With the goal of allowing writing and ideas to evolve and develop, over 1 to 2 weeks we do many writing exercises that lead to the final product, some of which I discuss below:

Descriptive Writing and Scenes of Memory

Using inspiration from DiYanni and Hoy's book, I structure multiple pathways for students to develop rich, descriptive writing that leads toward insights. For many, and especially for youth, inspiration comes from multiple modalities, including art and experience, not merely the written word. I model the way a concise, descriptive scene of memory from a student's life can be used as a powerful piece of evidence before asking students to brainstorm a list of memories that relate to the theme. I then give students a portion of class time to write a scene of memory, pushing them to write descriptively and what I describe as "in the moment so that readers can feel like they are there." This is a low-stakes writing assignment that students then share individually with classmates before I ask for volunteers to share their scenes with the large group. Writing and hearing these scenes advances students' thinking about the issues they are investigating and gets them closer to the development of compelling ideas. Encouraging students to incorporate these scenes into their academic writing opens a door for students to connect their lives to course content and explore complexity rather than searching for simple or overly general ideas to frame their writing. This is a shift from what would often otherwise be sterile writing based on a quote from a source that appeared early in a student's web search.

In addition to descriptive scenes, I use other in-class writing assignments to spark thinking and open doors to different types of analytical writing. In the unit on Violence, Militarism, and Alternatives, after we spent nearly 4 weeks reading and discussing the novel *The Things They Carried* (O'Brien, 1998), I project an iconic image taken at a Black Lives Matter protest in Baton Rouge in 2016 (Sidahmed, 2016). In the photo Iesha Evans stands rooted with strength and composure, facing a line of riot police, two of whom are charging toward her with handcuffs. As students open their notebooks, I describe the task: "Take 10 minutes and write a detailed description of what you see. Take the time to notice and describe as many details as possible. You may pay attention to body language, foreground and background, colors or textures, or other details." After students have written their descriptions, I ask volunteers to share excerpts of their writing. We hear multiple voices, mining the wisdom of the room to gather more and more details. "Those were excellent. Now, please huddle with your tablemates. What different ideas could emerge from a close examination of this photograph? Together, make a list of at least four ideas."

After about 8 minutes, I ask groups to share. I have asked a student to be the scribe at the board and am sitting on the edge of a windowsill off to the side of the room, intentionally placing myself outside of the center of the action. "There is definitely something about courage here. Doing what she is doing seems really hard," begins Tamir.

"At my table we were thinking about power. The police seem like they should have more power, but her posture doesn't show that," adds Sam.

The list of ideas grows. I occasionally offer a thought to help clarify or articulate a student idea but try to hang back, wanting student voices to be prioritized. When the time seems right for a transition I step back toward the front of the room.

"These are excellent! Nice job. Now, on your own, pick at least one of these ideas and think about how you can connect it to sources from different parts of the unit or to personal experience. Here's an example: If I pick the idea of courage in the face of violence, I can connect this to some of the different things we read over the last several weeks. For example, it relates to sections from *The Things They Carried* and some of what Gandhi wrote in *My Faith in Nonviolence* [an essay we had read and discussed the previous day] (Zinn, 2002). Finally, I could connect to a time when I left a protest because I was scared of the potential for violence." As I spoke, I drew a rough idea map on the board. "Now it's your turn. Take 10 minutes to draw a rough idea map of your own. This does not need to end up being your paper. You are just trying things out."

My last comments are designed to lower the stakes. Many students struggle with the early stages of writing, continually shutting themselves down because their "ideas aren't good," or they "don't like" what they have. To bypass these roadblocks, many of the early writing activities I structure are easy to conceptualize and access. I will give credit to students for completion rather than assigning a specific grade so that students are not penalized for taking risks and struggling with large ideas. This brings me back to the unit goals and the desire for students to see early steps as part of the process of discovery and creation of a polished final product.

Reading Sample Work and Reflecting on Earlier Writing

Rather than attempting to merely describe different characteristics of high-quality Advanced Essays, I create an assignment where they read and analyze essays from other students and published authors. Students record specific observations that they can point to in different parts of the writing and develop questions that they share with the class. These observations tend to be about writing style, technique, or the ways authors develop analysis or ideas. Sometimes the observations are surprising to me, as students notice details I overlooked but they found significant or important to consider in their own writing.

These activities allow students to think about their own preferences for writing styles and techniques while providing opportunities for me to consolidate their findings into guidelines that are clear enough for all students to have a sense of the goals for the paper. If a student continues to feel unclear about something on the rubric, such as "Essay smoothly moves between evidence, analysis, and development of larger idea or insights," the models are reference points that can be revisited.

Another strategy I use to help students develop their own writing goals is to have them revisit earlier work. Once we are several months into the year, I may ask them to look at multiple pieces of their writing. The assignment then is:

> Read over the essays and the feedback you received. Choose two excerpts where you are doing something interesting or important in your writing and two excerpts where there is something you could improve. Explanations should be a short paragraph that clearly explains your thinking and reflections on the excerpt.

I may then ask students to paste their writing goals at the top of their working doc and use these as conversation points when we conference about drafts.

Self-Evaluations and Peer Reviews of Drafts

While I believe deeply in the importance of conferencing with students about work in progress, I am also acutely aware of the challenge of doing this in a way that gives me reasonable amounts of class time to work with each student. By offering a structure for students to evaluate the state of their own work in progress and receive feedback from peers, I allow the work of feedback and revision to proceed without me. Additionally, by looking at the writing of their peers, students get additional ideas and inspiration for their own writing. However, these checkpoints can quickly lack substance if not designed to challenge students to be specific (and also kind).

Sometimes I structure these writing review activities around a handout for students to pass to reviewers once they share their docs with peers. At other times I list the specifics of the assignment on our online course management system and ask them to complete the work on their essay docs. At times the feedback seems to stand out more when it is written on a piece of paper that can be placed next to the device for revisions, and sometimes I prefer students to have everything in one place, with comments inserted directly on the working doc. This decision about process is one that I make based on a gut feeling of what might be most helpful for the most students at the time. I do this knowing that neither option will be executed smoothly by everyone.

Self-evaluations can be used as opportunities to have students compare their progress with project criteria and develop a work plan to move forward. Ideally, this process helps students strategize about revision. Questions for an Advanced Essay Self-Evaluation may include:

- In what ways does your evidence reveal new thinking about the issue you are investigating?
- Explain your current understanding of the larger idea you are developing in your paper.
- What parts of your writing feel strong? What parts do you need to revise, expand, or condense?

When structuring peer reviews, I am careful to include steps that validate the work of the author. Providing affirmation along with thoughtful feedback is something we work on throughout the year, but if it is not built into the process many students will receive feedback that will feel too much like personal criticism. This can easily cause students to become defensive or shut down and resist revision. For these reasons, peer reviewers are required to share ideas about the strong parts of the paper or what is working in the writing. Then they are to provide student authors with questions. This is something I regularly model in front of the class. There is a danger of reviewers offering directives or statements that can feel like insults. Often these ineffective comments start with the words "You should" or "You need to." Instead I coach students to offer questions such as "Can you explain this section more clearly?" or "Is there a way this connects with the previous part of the paper?" My experience is that any guideline that makes feedback into something the author can take in on their own terms helps young writers to be more open to revision and growth.

Sharing with the Group and Publishing to Blogs

When students complete their essays, we celebrate and collaborate. The day papers are due, students arrive to class and sit in a circle with the tables pushed to the side. I ask everyone to share an excerpt of their work, standing when they read, and have students offer snaps or claps as affirmations. After the readings I provide students a chance to recognize and affirm each other with shout-outs, reminding them to speak directly to the author of the paper as they commend the work. I also offer specific thoughts about what individual authors and the entire class accomplished. All these steps help to make the very individual work of writing a paper a more communal process that can be seen by students as an intellectual project supported by others. The students are not writing solely for the grade I will assign, because they are also creating something to be shared with their peers.

In addition to sharing in class, students post papers to their school blog. This step creates what feels like a more significant artifact of what they have written. Having their work online provides students, friends, and family with access to their writing. I tell students that they should be creating work that represents them well and that these papers can be used to publicly demonstrate their thinking and skills. Whenever a student asks me not to post to the web for personal or any other reason, my answer is always yes. My goal is not to force people to make public material that they want to be private, but to encourage students to share their work proudly and to create work that is worthy of wider audiences.

When students do post to their blogs, I ask them to write an Author's Note that serves to orient readers and provide an opportunity for reflection. Questions for the Author's Note include:

What were your goals for the essay? What are you proud of in the final product? What is one way you want to improve your writing process and/or writing technique for your next paper?

Much of the writing that my students produce in the Advanced Essay process is different from what people envision when they think of school essays. While some choose to stick with what they know, only slightly modifying the format of traditional academic essays, others find ways to use their lives and their city in their writing, creating profound and moving work. The result is writing that means something in the world, writing that has the potential to engage any reader, inside or outside of a classroom setting. My students' discoveries and insights speak to their investment in the process of crafting complex work. For example, Destiny used her essay to question the identities young people create on social media:

We start to believe in the lies we make up and lose our sense of reality. If you continue with the same lie, eventually you yourself believe that it is true. When lies make up our true identity, then do we really have a Self and is there really anything more than what's written on our social media bio?

Xu was able to understand his immigration experience in the context of different societal dynamics:

I was 4 years old when I first stepped foot in the United States. My mother told me that I was crying for the whole plane ride, and I did not stop until a couple of days later. My parents and I settled down in Kensington, in North Philadelphia. Other than going to school, I was not able to go outside because it was a really dangerous neighborhood.

Justin wrote about his insights from the transition from a homogenous private school to a diverse public school:

While it might sound odd that I am trying to defend myself as someone who went to a private school, looking back on myself as a person during those 10 years, I don't see a snobby rich white kid. I do see a sheltered white kid. . . . As the [new] community began to accept me for who I was, I was not only taught that being a white kid in a school with other white kids caused me to be unaware of racial issues such as stereotyping and racial profiling, but it taught me that it was better to not grow up in a sheltered environment.

Being at SLA, I realized that I used to be completely oblivious to how our society treats minorities so horribly. Although, the main issue in my eyes was that I practically had no friends outside of my race at my old school, and I was not aware of what it was like to be the minority.

As it turns out, this experiment with writing instruction not only helped my students write with more insight and passion but also helped me develop an idea of my own: How we ask students to write affects their understandings of learning and creation. I am left with the belief that curriculum designed with the intention of bringing more meaning to the work of school lets students explore ideas, express themselves, and create in compelling, innovative, and public ways.

MODERN-DAY DE TOCQUEVILLES

Several years ago, I began planning a unit for an 12th-grade U.S. Government class. I knew that the unit would be on the theme of democracy but in the beginning of my planning process the specific learning goals were unclear. I began to research, looking for texts that could be part of the unit, but also educating myself and looking for model work that could be used within the unit. I spoke to other teachers, friends, and scholars, making sure my search for relevant content was wider than the top hits in a web search. I visited libraries and spent time in bookstores and online. As I described previously, this early stage of unit design can be overwhelming, but it is also an energizing opportunity to engage one's self as a scholar and to be reimmersed in the joy of discovering new content and ideas. I enjoy following the jagged path of my thinking and my own inquiry during these periods as I read, watch, reflect, and learn from others. This process of exploration is a way many teachers renew enthusiasm for the the content they teach.

I regularly save articles and sources that may relate to my teaching with a social bookmarking app. These apps are a useful way to organize resources and sort curriculum ideas using tags you create. You can share these collections of links with others, including groups of students. Reviewing sources I had previously tagged with the word *democracy* helped me think about different definitions of democracy and propelled my thinking for the unit. I reread an article which argues that issues of race point to larger problems in democracy in the United States (Guinier & Torres, 2015). A friend had once recommended the documentary *The Democratic Promise: Saul Alinsky and His Legacy* (Baldwin et al., 1999). I had previously tagged it and now watched it. The film describes democracy as an ongoing process, an understanding I realized I wanted my students to develop during the unit.

I began to settle on unit goals to frame the learning. During the unit I wanted students to:

- Develop an understanding of democracy as more than a political system
- Investigate the state of democracy in the United States

These goals would mean that in the unit students would develop knowledge that was relevant to their lives and critically examine society. My hope was that these goals would provide students both a context and motivation for discovering new information about our country, and would help them question a concept (democracy) that is often spoken of without clear meaning or understanding (Baldwin et al., 1999).

At this point I had my goals and an accumulated collection of sources, so I began crafting Essential Questions (EQs) that would frame the inquiry (McTighe & Wiggins, 2013). I kept the number of EQs small so the unit would have coherence. Writing questions that were open but would also steer us in the right direction was (and always is) a challenge. I settled on:

- What is the history of democracy in the United States?
- In what different ways can we take the democratic pulse of our nation?
- In what ways can a deep investigation of specific topics lead to larger, complex insights about democracy and the country we live in?

The third EQ related to my evolving plan for a culminating project and my desire for students to direct their own learning in the later stages of the unit. I find it important to connect the culminating project to the heart of the unit rather than having it emerge as something extra that doesn't connect to the essence of what we have been investigating. As with most of my units, my plan was for the class to begin the inquiry together. We would spend more than 2 weeks reading and watching sources as students wrote journal entries and discussed, allowing them to develop and share rough ideas. Then students would begin a more extended process of creating work of their own. The project part of the unit would include many mini-lessons and both modeling and sharing of work, but this section would be driven by the ideas students were exploring and work they were creating.

I decided to begin by having students examine their own thinking and understandings about democracy and then contrast this with a range of definitions and ideas about the concept. This exercise would help them to discover complexity while they realized that democracy is a word and a concept that many people use without a clear meaning and also provide a rationale for work we would do later in the unit. I designed an *Investigation of Democracy* activity that students would complete. They began by drawing a sketch that represented some aspect of their understanding of the meaning of democracy. After sharing sketches with a group, they would list what they understood to be democratic values. Finally, they would read a list of quotations about democracy that I had curated and rank the statements in order of (their opinion of) increasing accuracy, while attempting to arrive at consensus on their own definition of democracy. I knew that this consensus would be nearly impossible. My true goal was for them to begin to understand democracy as a disputed concept that can encompass multiple meanings.

I then crafted journal entries that would be used to start different classes in the unit and push students to realize different things that would help them with their later investigation. I made a question sheet to go with *The Democratic Promise* film and designed activities to go with some of the other readings I had found. I was getting excited! I could see the potential for students to connect with the content in meaningful ways, ways that would matter to them.

What I needed to pull it all together and give the unit clear direction and purpose was the final project. Alexis de Tocqueville's book *Democracy in America* resonated with me because of its insightful yet short and accessible chapters. As a Frenchman examining the state of democracy in the United States in the 1800s, de Tocqueville had asked many questions and investigated many different topics. This was exactly what I wanted my students to do. I designed an activity where students would read selected chapters and see that his investigation of democracy included a focus on issues of gender, inequality, religion, patriotism, and race, among other topics.

As I puzzled over how to best frame the reasons for reading this work from nearly 2 centuries ago and thought about ways students could critique de Tocqueville's work, I stumbled across my idea—students could be Modern-Day de Tocquevilles! By using his work as a model, students could do contemporary investigations of different aspects of democracy, asking questions, doing original research, writing short chapters, and creating multimedia to accompany the text. One goal for the project was to offer choices to students as they conducted research and then designed a product. The expectation was that their final products would develop complex, intellectually rigorous ideas and understandings.

Put together, student chapters could be posted on a website that would be our own updated version of the book *Democracy in America*. My students could even create their own Modern-Day de Tocqueville names, such as "Marcus from Uptown," an example of a name a student did use for his final project. I hoped that the work would be engaging to those beyond the walls of the classroom as well as shared with and celebrated by their peers. I wanted to be able to share the final product widely on social media and maybe even entice some reporters to write about young people's perspectives on democracy in America. I could use this extra goal to further motivate students to create the highest-quality work possible.

Completing the projects would take several weeks, and I would have to create many intermediate deadlines. I knew that students would be excited by the multimedia components but that the challenging intellectual work would take place in the researching and writing of the chapters. I organized the schedule so that each chapter's text component had to be completed before students could begin work on the accompanying multimedia. I wanted the process to be individual but also have an ethos of collaboration. This meant that students would be reviewing each other's work and I would conference with students regularly, paying close attention to students who were struggling and figuring out what they needed to succeed on such an ambitious project. I would also have to tune in to those who were progressing quickly, making sure to ask them strategic questions that would deepen their work and having them give and receive peer feedback along the way. As a final step in my unit design, I connected the plan to state standards, a simple step for a unit that contained many different texts, literacy activities, and concepts about United States government and society.

Below is the project description that I shared with the students. As with all my projects, I made the description as clear and brief as possible and built it upon readings we had already done, previous class discussions, and work students had already completed. The list of possible questions for further evaluation was taken from student responses in an earlier assignment when students had analyzed de Tocqueville's work. The description also included links to resources I curated for students.

Modern-Day de Tocqueville Book Assignment

Goal: To present detailed observations and analysis about the state of democracy in America today

One Chapter: 750 words + multimedia + citations

Multimedia: Photos you take, video or audio you create, infographics you create, or another idea you get approved

Possible questions for investigation (these can be used as chapter titles):

- Take any chapter title from the original work and write a modern-day version of it.
- How do people in the United States view their past? How do they view their government and country today?
- Has democracy in the United States lost meaning throughout time?
- Is the United States an oligarchy?
- What is the role of civil disobedience in a democracy?
- What is the reality of homelessness in the United States?

- What are different views about guns in the United States?
- What is the relationship between race and wealth?
- Should the structure of elections and representation change?
- Is confrontation necessary for social change?
- What prevents people from working for change?
- What different social movements currently exist in United States society?
- What is the reality of poverty in the United States?
- What does democracy look like from an immigrant perspective?
- What are the real implications of unequal school funding?
- What is the role of prisons in United States society? [Abridged list]

Figure 2.1 is the rubric that accompanied the project, although, as with all my projects, the complete picture of expectations was presented through a collective classroom examination and analysis of model work. I generally choose to include only one category on rubrics so that students know what to aim for but are not overwhelmed by a large amount of text in multiple cells.

The learning in this unit had the potential to redefine students' understanding of themselves and the world. Ron, a student in a class that did this project, described this as he reflected on his learning experiences, "One thing that I've learned about myself is that I can articulate how I feel in a very solid sense and that other people will listen . . . I finally realized I have a voice and I can use it. And that feels good" (Schwartz, 2015). (Links to final products and other project materials in Appendix.)

CODA

The examples in this chapter reveal that, rather than a circumscribed set of guidelines for planning units and designing transformational learning experiences, there is a jagged, uneven, rich path that allows educators to discover and create in response to local circumstances. This pathway and the process of designing curriculum is one of the joys of teaching—it is intellectual, challenging, and creative. Just this week, a book about the history of xenophobic rhetoric in the United States and a conversation with a friend led me to a search for sources about U.S. intervention in Latin America and impacts of the climate crisis on migration as I began generating goals for a new unit. This unit will be different from what I

Figure 2.1. Modern-Day Alexis de Tocqueville Books: Rubric

Design	Chapter is well organized with a clear question, a clear, sophisticated argument, and smooth transitions.
Knowledge	Sources present important evidence and are accompanied by complex analysis.
Application	The combination of outside sources and multimedia create an engaging investigation of the topic.
Presentation	Layout is creative and clear. The writing is polished, persuasive, and specific. The chapter is an extension of the original work of Alexis de Tocqueville. Multimedia is smoothly integrated with text and is less than 2 minutes long (if video or audio).
Process	Deadlines are met and time is used productively.

would have designed 10 years ago or what I would teach with a different group of students.

My design process is regularly influenced by what I observe to be the needs of a group and my awareness of the importance of providing a range of learning experiences throughout a semester. Often my process begins with an external source, such as a book, film, or exhibition, that sparks an idea. There is no well-organized diagram that I can offer to help someone design curriculum for deeper learning. Educators can seek outside inspiration, tap into local resources, prioritize student creation, and observe student lives and classroom dynamics. What is clear is that deep learning occurs when student work is rooted in compelling, challenging issues and focuses on topics and themes that stimulate and affirm students, pushing them to dig deeply, discovering new ideas and insights.

CHAPTER 3

Elevating Student Voices and Truths

The pitcher cries for water to carry and a person for work that is real.

—Marge Piercy, 2002

It was a bitterly cold Wednesday morning in the middle of January. Outside, our city felt gray and harsh. The energy in the hallways before the school day began was lacking. My student teacher and I rushed to push our classroom tables off to the sides and put the chairs in a large, inward-facing circle before the students entered. They began to trickle through the doorway as we got the last chairs into formation. "Good morning, Xavier. How's it going? Hey Kobe, good to see you. Take a seat in the circle." I make a point of greeting students individually, often checking in briefly with them in the process. I want students to feel recognized the minute they walk in my room, and I also want to make connections. If someone looks or sounds out of sorts, I will reach out further, hoping to learn more and find ways to offer support and affirmation.

The week had been hard. No one seemed to have energy for school or for much of anything as winter bore down on us. The students in this 11th-grade English class had been working on their third Advanced Essay of the year, focusing on themes of identity and belonging. The drafts students had been writing and revising seemed to be progressing slowly. My writing conferences with students and what I heard while eavesdropping on student conversations during peer reviews left me with a lot of concerns. My student teacher and I had been strategizing regularly, trying to figure out ways to infuse energy into the class and adjust the course of the path we found ourselves heading down.

"Good morning, everybody. Thanks for being on time on this gray day." I spoke to the circle of students, many of whom did not seem to be fully present as their bodies slumped in different directions in the circle around me. After reminding them of our current goal of producing writing that used scenes of memory (short, written snapshots from their lives) to get to unique ideas or insights about identity or belonging, I asked everyone to prepare to share some of their work, "Please go to your paper and choose your favorite one or two paragraphs to read out loud. We're going to hear something from everyone."

There was some muttering and a couple of groans, but everyone flipped up their laptop screens and prepared themselves. I braced myself for what I believed was going to be a torturous 30 minutes. After giving students a couple minutes, I spoke again: "I want to remind everyone that it is challenging and scary to share one's work in public. I always feel the same thing when I share my own work. For this reason, it's your responsibility to support your classmates. When someone stands to read, show them you are listening. When people are reading, the only screens that should be up are the person reading and the person next to them getting ready. After someone reads, show support and snap." I paused to look around the circle. The prospect of reading work out loud had woken many people up but it was still unclear how the morning would unfold. "Who's going first?" I asked.

Without hesitation Nadya stood, laptop resting in her hands. She had emailed me at some point during the night, letting me know she hadn't completed her final draft. I hoped that she would start us off on a positive note but sat toward the front edge of my chair, not knowing how it would go. I knew Nadya as someone who was often comfortable voicing complex ideas in discussions, but she regularly faced struggles converting her ideas into writing. Her nearly full-time work schedule after school and the fact that I had to regularly nudge her to persevere through multiple drafts until her ideas came through clearly in writing meant that the work she submitted often seemed quite rough. As she read, I was caught off guard by her confidence:

> I hear it every day, we hear it every day. We are not here to be successful; the world of education is not made for us. By us I mean kids in situations that not everybody faces, kids who haven't had the advantages most other kids have. These kids are deprived a rightful education from this current education system. We are enrolled in these classes but not much learning happens in these classrooms. Ds dramatically placed down upon a paper every marking period. Teachers passing along the river of trouble to the next available teacher.

The audience was with her, murmuring assent. She sat. Students snapped. The air and the energy in the room began to shift. Without me saying anything, Samir stood and began:

"You boys know if I could afford it I wouldn't hesitate to get it. I don't like saying no and making you sad." This was something we always heard from our mom if we couldn't afford any luxuries and the week we would be facing was going to be a tight one.

"We know mom." I knew the majority of our money went to bills and food. We did need the essentials, after all. While sometimes we do live paycheck to paycheck, we aren't poor. It's just our bills that decide to try to pull us under for a few moments. But somehow we make it through. We budget and save, budget and save to make sure we have enough money to do things we want.

Powerful snaps came from the group. Then Jimmy stood and began:

Who would say being born from two undocumented immigrants would be such a hassle? So much pressure on my shoulders, looking for opportunities they missed out on. Learning the dominant language in the country, English. My parents don't even want to teach me about our culture, I mean their culture. Americanization is what decided my name, my mother and father thought James was a perfect name for a non-white kid could have to fit in in order meet their expectations. However they gave me their last name to also show I'm Latino. Saldivar not pronounced Salvador or Saldevar. James or Jimmy that's what I go by now.

"These are really good," Madison said under her breath as others snapped and William began reading. The day was shaping up differently from how it began. Student voices and the perspectives of young people filled the space, creating a new reality of investigation, testimony, and ideas affirmed by the audience. One after another, students read work that was interesting, insightful, and often poignant. The class was in it together, supporting each other and appreciating the creations of their peers. While it was clear that the products left room for improvement, there was impressive work to celebrate. Students, many of whom had histories of struggling academically, had found ways to integrate person-al experience along with quotes from outside sources to develop com-plex, important ideas about identity and belonging. I had been carrying around nagging frustration and doubts during the previous week as I thought about the work and the different ways students were struggling. Sitting in this circle, listening to students confidently read and then receive affirmations, I got a different sense of what we had accomplished and why it is important for the work of school to be communally shared and publicly acknowledged.

After everyone read, I asked if anyone wanted to offer any specific shout-outs or comments on the work. I reminded students to speak directly to one another, telling about details they appreciated within the excerpts. After many shout-outs were shared, Samir raised his hand. I nodded to him to speak. "I just want to say how proud I am of everyone here. Those papers are really smart. We did good work." There were smiles, some high fives, and exclamations all around. No one was paying any mind to the January weather.

***

Creating a classroom that can shift learners' understandings of the world and themselves requires educators to reexamine academic practices that support superficial understandings of learning and instead structure school in ways that affirm human needs of recognition and connection. This chapter examines different pathways for elevating student voices and truths within schools. Teachers can work to create these types of transgressive, participatory learning experiences by acknowledging and honoring students' realities, building cohesive classroom communities, making learning complex and real, and decentralizing the classroom while prioritizing student voices.

ACKNOWLEDGING AND HONORING STUDENTS' REALITIES

I once taught a student who spent months struggling with depression and cutting. One day, I watched her stand up in front of the class and share a poem that she'd written about facing her struggles. When she finished, the class erupted with cheers and calls of "You go!" and "That's right!" The student walked back to her seat attempting to conceal her smile and pride.

In the fall of 2014, after the class read Michelle Alexander's essay *Telling My Son About Ferguson* (2014) together, I listened as a group of students from different backgrounds, some with memories of traumatic

experiences at the hands of police officers and others with police officers in their families, shared responses to the death of Michael Brown.
The room was filled with sadness, fear, and hurt as students disagreed,
yelled, and cried, but also heard each other. I will never forget what it
was like for us all to listen to Joy, speaking to the class with her hand
over her face as she began to cry: "I hate this stuff. It makes me really
angry! Makes me not want to have kids."

The other day, a student dragged his feet as he slowly entered my
classroom, having made multiple trips during the night between his home
and the 24-hour pharmacy. He had been trying to get the medicine for
his father's cancer treatment but had continually run into bureaucratic
obstacles symptomatic of a dysfunctional health care system.

Years ago, when I spoke to a student whose grades and engagement
in class had dropped dramatically during December, I learned that her
family's heat had been cut off. She was unsure when her family would
have the money to pay the gas bill in order to get it turned back on.
Another year, I learned that a student had been living without electricity
for months. She had become accustomed to doing her homework and
putting on her makeup by flashlight.

I share these examples not because they are exceptional nor for dra-
matic effect. Rather, they illustrate some of the ways that students in
our society come to school with burdens, trauma, and unresolved issues.
Celebrating the potential of young people and the power of democratic
education means acknowledging and understanding the different ways
that our society falls short. Believing in education and in human potential requires acknowledgment of inequalities that are ingrained in the
fabric of our society. Being an educator means meeting people where
they are and helping them understand themselves, their lived realities,
our society, and the world.

In our country, where there is enormous educational inequity, teaching contexts differ drastically. In some teaching contexts, many students
may arrive at school not having had their basic needs met. At the other
end of the spectrum, many students come from environments steeped in
vapid materialism and overconsumption. While educators and activists
work for structural change, we can seek to challenge and nurture young
people, pushing a range of students to develop their own understandings
of social change and possibility.

Unequal schools and the disparate daily realities of students are a reminder that educators must develop pedagogy that speaks to and examines different understandings and experiences. To ignore young people's

lives and current social realities is to fail students and miss the potential for education to inform, challenge, and inspire change. There is work to be done in all classroom settings—exclusive institutions, high-poverty areas, mixed-population schools, and environments not easily summarized. The work differs depending on the community and the individuals. The work of consciousness raising is as necessary for those raised within insular backgrounds of privilege as it is for those who struggle at the margins of our society.

The lives of adolescents are complex. Learning is most powerful when educators acknowledge this complexity and find different ways to make space for it within the classroom and the work that students produce. One pathway for acknowledging and honoring students' realities is to use aspects of students' lives as starting points for inquiry. Years ago a veteran Philly teacher, Marsha Pincus, introduced me to the idea of "language autobiographies." The project requires students to see their world and their identities in new ways (Cook-Sather, 2009). With this project as inspiration, I designed a unit that requires students to interrogate systems of language, power, and identity while creating work that allows them to analyze and respond to their life experiences. Part of my intention in sharing this unit is to offer an example of how technology can be strategically utilized to deepen the intellectual experiences of learners within the framework of teaching for a living democracy.

The unit began with me asking the students their thoughts about one of the essential questions for the unit: "What are the relationships among language, power, and identity?" My goal was to open up these concepts as complex areas worthy of exploration and investigation. Students had time to journal and record initial thoughts before we discussed these concepts that relate to all of our lives. Students wrote about relatives with strong accents or dialects and being judged for the ways they speak, among other topics. At this point in the process their ideas are interesting but not very developed. These beginning stages are a little bit like tilling the soil in preparation for the work that lies ahead.

I then told the students that we were about to begin reading a book that was written in a rural, Southern, African American dialect in the 1930s. I asked who had been to the South and who had been exposed to Southern dialects. Many of my students shared stories of visiting relatives or told of relatives who migrated to the North as part of the Great Migration. Others reported that they had no connection to or experiences with these types of dialects.

For the next several weeks we immersed ourselves in *Their Eyes Were Watching God* by Zora Neale Hurston (2006). As we were nearing the end of the novel we returned to the idea of language as a topic for investigation. One way we did this was by creating a class dictionary in which students shared words or phrases that mattered to them. My hope was that this dictionary would help recenter perceptions of dialects and personalized ways of speaking. Instead of seeing what some call non-standard English as a wrong way of speaking, I wanted students to see and experience the creativity and unique forms of expression and meaning inherent in different ways of speaking. On an online forum I wrote:

> Share two words that matter to you. They can be slang, a word only used by you and those close to you, have to do with your family or your home language, or may be unique to Philly.

Students were enthusiastic about posting to our class dictionary and incorporated teenage slang, words from different languages, and jokes that they share with their friends. Some sample student responses:

> *That's dead*: It doesn't matter, end of conversation.
> *Schemin'*: Someone who lies about the truth.
> *Salty Grits*: When someone is wrong/incorrect.
> *Doing the most*: When someone is unnecessarily doing too much.

An online forum where everyone submitted concurrently allowed for a wider range of responses than a discussion where the first respondents set the tone for an entire group. Additionally, student voices that are not always present within group discussions often seem to more successfully contribute to online sharing.

For the next step I gave students the assignment to "write a prose scene about a real event in order to show some part of your language identity." Students wrote the scenes one night and the next day posted them to a separate forum for their classmates to see. As students read each other's scenes they began to create lists of issues related to language. As a class we continued to discuss ideas of language, power, and identity.

The use of a digital forum to share student writing allowed the class to continue a process of inquiry. Students were able to look at the writing from the class as a whole and notice patterns that emerged. No one piece was prioritized over any other, providing space for the development of unique, individual voices, opinions, and ideas. I made a point of complimenting the unique features of multiple scenes in order to affirm students who had chosen to approach the assignment creatively.

The next week was spent reading essays from different authors about their experiences with language. James Baldwin, bell hooks, Gloria Anzaldúa, and Mike Rose helped the students to develop a rich understanding of the complexity and poignancy of our topics. As students' vocabularies and understandings of the issues began to grow, students from varied backgrounds began to reexamine many aspects of their own daily realities. Students began to distinguish between slang and Black English or African American Vernacular. They began to articulate some of the ways that their most intimate languages allow them to express themselves and connect with others in unique and personalized ways and recognized that many of these languages are judged harshly by mainstream society. Students discussed and debated the merits of code switching as a necessary skill for survival (Auer, 2013). There was a collective acknowledgment of the connection between language and power and the hegemony of and lack of emotion associated with Standard English.

Finally, it was time for the students to write their own language autobiographies. We began crafting the papers. I made a conscious decision not to reveal anything about the multimedia component that would follow with the knowledge that many students find it easier to immerse themselves in a media project and there was potential that they would do so at the expense of the ideas they were developing in the papers. It seems that when given the option, most students will gravitate to multimedia work in lieu of what can feel like the more demanding work of intellectual discovery. I wanted to make sure that complex ideas were developed before the creation of the digital product began.

Students brought in drafts, the class discussed different themes and methods of analysis, peers edited each other's work, and eventually most students were ready to submit polished final products. It was then that I told students that their final papers (which they already knew were going to be public) were to be posted to their blogs along with a digital story that would present material that was similar to or complementary to the paper. "Digital stories use still images, narration, and words on the screen to communicate larger ideas," I explained. We screened several sample digital stories and dissected different aspects of the form before the students took over the process.

As is often the case, the media production drew in almost all the students. The excitement could be felt in the room as I described this step.

Often, even students who do not commit themselves fully to a written paper fully dedicate themselves to a media project. The challenge is to channel the excitement and eagerness into the specific details required to produce quality final products.

All students were responsible for creating a script that matched narration to images. When their scripts were ready, they called me over and talked me through their plans before I sent them off to record and edit. I used this opportunity to ask clarifying questions and point out areas for revision with the hope of helping all students improve their scripts. With some students our conversation entailed clarifying the larger idea or flow of ideas in their script. With others, the discussion was more about technical details such as how many outside quotes to include while still managing to maintain viewer interest.

While most students embraced this stage of the process, others were quickly frustrated with technological challenges. I checked in with these students frequently and tried to help them find allies who could help them troubleshoot challenges that arose. For 2 days I circulated around the room as a consultant, answering questions about details and reminding students to take the time to recheck and polish their final products so that they could proudly share them with a wider audience.

In many ways, the digital stories are what transformed insightful papers into living documents of students' realities, struggles, and transformations. In her paper, *Beyond Translating* (2012), Ellen wrote:

> Ever since I could talk, I was assigned the role of translator in my family. Every time I go over to my grandparents' house, I am a *Dizú* to Cantonese translator for my grandma and grandpa . . . .
>
> It was a cold winter morning when I woke up before the sun with my dad. We left the house while it was still pitch black out. We talked about how he always had to wake up so early and go to work every Sunday . . . I walked to the Whole Foods Sushi Department. When I got there, I stood at the entrance watching my dad work and shred through the salmon, seaweed, and rice with his hands and a sushi blade. While he is doing that a customer walks up to the counter and starts asking my dad questions. PANIC MODE.
>
> "Excuse me? What's the difference in these two rolls?" She says as she gestures to the Dragon roll and the Spider roll.
>
> "Daddy, *kueh yew gee gaw long gah roll yow meh yeah yup*

been ah . . . [Daddy, she wants to know what is in each roll.] I say quickly and quietly as he walks toward her.

"I know, *noi noi.*" He said all confidently.

"Oh . . . okay daddy." That's when I realized that my parents are in their everyday job and they don't need me to defend them here.

"The dragon roll inside eel, cucumber. Outside is avocado. On top avocado. And spider roll outside have masago. Inside has soft-shell crab, snow crab, and avocado." He says with an accent.

Then my dad walks back with a satisfied face and says: "*Gnaw sick gnaw jogan meh yeah! A yah noi noi.* [I know what I am doing and saying, daughter. Oh gosh daughter.]"

Nevertheless, that's one memory that will most likely have me questioning the fact that my parents don't need me as a translator as much as I thought they do as the years pass by. It's a saddening thought that keeps getting bigger and bigger but I guess it'll get easier as I write it on paper? I hope so. Just the thought of losing the one thing that I have done to help them so much is heart breaking because they've done so much for me and for me to lose that role is like losing a lifetime job.

Ellen's paper is a powerful narrative of a first-generation immigrant youth continually learning to navigate different worlds. Her work gains additional power, poignancy, and individualization as a result of the digital story that she made to accompany the paper. The viewer can hear the voices of the many different members of the family as they introduce themselves in their native tongues and Ellen performs her longstanding role as family translator. (Links to the full paper and digital story are in Appendix section A.) Put together, the paper, the digital story, and the introduction she wrote at the beginning of her blog post create a power-ful document of learning that appeals to a wider audience. The complex ideas and poignant emotion provide a rationale for posting the work on the web and sharing it widely.

Overall, the design of this unit motivated students to apply intel-lectual frameworks to issues that integrally connect to their identities. There was high student engagement and investment in the opportunity to develop ideas about their own realities, which connected to deeper issues involving language and power. This was an opportunity to make their work public and tell their stories in varied and creative ways.

BUILDING COHESIVE CLASSROOM COMMUNITIES

Teachers spend hundreds of classroom hours with students. During the cycles of a school year and the daily, overfull minutes of class periods, it is challenging to do the complex work of building meaningful community and trusting, supportive relationships. This is the work that makes teaching such an exhausting, rewarding, and unique endeavor. This is also the work that can never be scripted and that individuals pursue differently.

In the regular, seemingly endless and often fraught work involved in building classroom community I find it helpful to renew my vision by returning to aspects of Martin Luther King Jr.'s "beloved community," a key element of which is that "Love and trust will triumph over fear and hatred." In addition, King acknowledged that conflict is "an inevitable part of human experience" (King Center, n.d.).

It is quite challenging to find ways to be an available, supportive presence in the midst of jam-packed school days, yet there is no question that classrooms that function as communities support deep learning and lay the groundwork for authentic experiences. Teachers can remind themselves to speak intentionally to classes and students, being sure to find ways to connect as unique individuals rather than merely as people compelled to be in the same place. This can mean setting a tone that is consistently welcoming, appreciative, and caring. It also means responding to students in human-centered, rather than mechanistic, ways. Functioning communities encourage people to be present and to contribute. Teachers can plan for students to have regular, daily opportunities to express themselves and share ideas, both with each other in smaller groups and in the larger communal setting. It is through the use of strategies and intentional behaviors that teachers can create truly student-oriented communities.

Caring for young people is often a primary reason that adults choose to teach, yet it can be very difficult to develop a practice where deep appreciation for students is regularly communicated. I am so often focused on what I want my students to achieve and on how they, and I, can improve what we are doing that I forget to acknowledge successes that are happening right in front of me. Everyone gains from public acknowledgment of what is going well, high-quality work, and insightful comments. By reminding myself to focus on what is good in my classroom, even at the times when I feel like it is much easier to identify struggles, I am able to shift the ethos of our community to one of acknowledgment and celebration.

Assuming a stance of acknowledging good is part of a larger role of playing the role of host and working to set a positive tone in the room. Even on days when I've had to race to school after a chaotic morning at home and feel like less than my best self, my students deserve to feel welcomed and valued. The more kindness, warmth, and compassion that I convey, the more students will learn, grow, and connect. I want my students to know when I feel that they've fallen short or can do better, but I strive to make sure that these challenges come in the context of support and belief in their abilities. Earlier in my career I saw my role as primarily connected to curriculum and intellectual growth. These days I am also aware of the different ways my actions can contribute to building the climate that draws young people toward the intellectual work.

One way to discover and honor student realities is to make checking in a regular part of the work of teaching. I get consumed thinking about content and projects, making it is easy for me to forget how my students' minds are already busy with thoughts that don't relate to my class when they arrive in the classroom. Small gestures of acknowledgment and connection often have a large impact on the energy and mood and life of a group. Sometimes this means checking in with individual students via short conversations at the door, or starting class by asking people how they are and having volunteers share bits of news. It gives us a short transition time together where we reconnect as individuals and challenge aspects of compulsory schooling that do not communicate to students that they are valued as people. Another form of checking in is via conferences, discussed in the next chapter.

Student Collaboration

Sharing my rough writing with others can be a miserable experience. While I know that outside input is a crucial part of revision, I feel my discomfort rise as others make comments and probe with questions. Inevitably, I begin to feel resentment grow as I am forced to reevaluate passages that I thought were clear. If collaboration feels this challenging for me with those whom I trust and respect, it must feel even harder for my students because I often make a point of dividing them into heterogeneous groups that include students with different academic skill levels. These groupings ensure that struggling students will have student helpers or mentors nearby and that those who are adept at navigating academic requirements will develop skills and compassion required to work with people different from them. The projects I assign require coordination among all the members of a group. I remind students that the path to success requires effective collaboration among group members although students will take on different roles depending on their comfort level with different skills.

Despite these difficulties, I believe that it would be a huge mistake to teach in a way that did not emphasize collaboration. Each year, as a result of different collaborative experiences, my classroom is transformed from a random collection of individuals into a supportive learning community. The collective effort and exchange of ideas lead to final products and understandings that would not be possible if students were working in isolation.

Learning is a social process, and the learning process is deepened when ideas are challenged and learners are pushed to produce work that surpasses their expectations of what they can do. But, since working in groups is continually challenging, it is important that students aren't obliged to work together on projects where collaboration is not necessary or beneficial to the final product. People do not benefit from a collective process when there are not enough tasks to be shared. For example, the final stages of video or audio editing generally take place on one device. Being aware of this, I design these projects for individuals or partners to complete or make it so individual group members must each create their own component that then becomes part of a larger whole.

Communities thrive when people have voice and when they're given opportunities to communicate with others. When work is a collaborative endeavor (even if the final product is individual), there are opportunities to connect with and learn from others. Sherry Turkle provides us with a thoughtful reminder about the value of face-to-face conversation and how it differs from communication that happens with technology: "[W]e need to remember...to listen to one another, even to the boring bits, because it is often in unedited moments, moments in which we hesitate and stutter and go silent, that we reveal ourselves to one another" (Turkle, 2012).

Collaborative relationships between and among students are the result of intentional effort, careful planning, modeling, and facilitation. I am frequently reminded that collaboration is a learned skill and that if I don't take regular, intentional steps it can become dysfunctional, more of a detriment to the community than behaviors that connect students. Asking students to reflect on previous collaborative experiences before joining a group can be an opportunity for classes to share ideas and strategies, creating guidelines for the entire group.

Peer Feedback

On the second week of our playwriting projects (see Appendix section A) students come in having written three rough scenes. It is early in the process and, despite having read sample scenes together, discussed different features and qualities of plays, and shared prewriting with the class, students are unsure. I make a point of speaking to Marina at the door as she enters:

> "Your scenes are great! Can your work be a model to share with the class?"
>
> Her mouth is smiling but in her eyes I can see an expression of fear. "Really?" she asks, clearly on the fence about whether to say yes.
>
> "Yes. You got this." I respond quickly, hoping my positive energy will seal the deal.
>
> After everyone is settled, I begin class.
>
> "Good morning. Really good to see everyone. Show me with your thumb, either up, down, or in the middle, how was it to write your scenes?"
>
> I look around the room at the range of responses, trying to make sure that everyone can see that almost everyone is acknowledging that the writing was challenging.
>
> "All right. I want to remind you that plays are written to be performed. In a way, your play isn't real until it is heard by others. Also, once you hear your own play out loud, you will immediately begin getting ideas for revision. In a minute, we're going to hear a scene from Marina's play. Before we do, I want to remind you of a couple things. First, it is scary to hear your work out loud. Remember to honor and respect the author. Audience, as you listen, you need to be taking notes of things that are working well and areas for revision. I'm going to call on you to share pluses and questions. Remember that no one gets to tell an author what to do, but you can offer questions to help with revision. The author gets to decide if your feedback will strengthen their work. Marina, you'll be recording all the pluses and questions on your doc. Everybody ready? Let's move the chairs to set up our theater seating. Marina, have you shared your doc with your actors?"

There are several things I emphasize as we begin what during this project will be a regular process of writing, sharing, receiving feedback, and revising. I maintain these goals for much of what we do together and see them as part of my work of community building. Students should feel that their work is part of a larger process of creation that is supported collectively. They should feel that others in the room are interested in their work and invested in them succeeding in creating something meaningful. By making feedback a collaborative process that will later continue in small groups, students develop an awareness of possibility and the potential to be inspired and encouraged by their peers. In addition to benefiting the author of the work that is discussed, this process exposes others to additional model work, ideally providing inspiration or a path forward for those that need it. The result is that work is being created and revised in community and students develop a stake in the work of their peers.

Norms of Compassion and Flexibility

Ultimately, classroom communities where students are willing to take risks and create work that is deeply meaningful to them are compassionate places. Compassionate classroom environments are not environments that lack academic rigor. In a compassionate environment, students are understood to be complex people. Here, young people feel that they belong. Here, they feel challenged and encouraged while we ask them to be the best versions of themselves.

The ways teachers frame academic challenges also greatly impact the dynamics of a class. It is important to set high expectations while expressing confidence that students can succeed with tasks that may feel overwhelming. On a group project, I may remind a class, "This is challenging, but if you work together and use your time wisely, you will be able to create something impressive." At other times, early in the process of creation I may say, "There is no way to do this wrong. As long as you are getting ideas down on the page you are in good shape."

I push, but I am also cautious. If I push them beyond what is possible, students will rebel and refuse to challenge themselves. I try to work toward a place where they need to stretch but will not feel that they are going to break. This is an unchoreographed dance that occurs when I speak to the group but also in individual check-ins and the ways I adapt assignments for different students. I need to continually remember the importance of being flexible while also maintaining an elevated vision of success. When students do not succeed, I make it clear to them that while I hoped for more, I know that everyone messes up. I find that this balance of rigor and understanding is key to students feeling that they belong in and are seen as part of the class.

MAKING LEARNING COMPLEX AND REAL

When curriculum and classroom practice is framed around inquiry, the status quo is open to examination and debate. Susan Lytle, a professor and author whom I count as a mentor, speaks regularly of the importance of problematizing and troubling ideas. This stance of searching out complexity and thoughtful paths of exploration is a key element of designing units of study and classroom practices that help students develop the intellectual feistiness to question what many of us have learned to accept as given.

Essential Questions

Nonviolence activist George Lakey writes about the importance of framing learning in order to increase participation (Lakey, 2010). In school settings this framing can be accomplished through the use of Essential Questions to initiate inquiry (McTighe & Wiggins, 2013). EQs provide a framework for investigation and establish pathways for students to focus on topics where there are problems, tension, or struggle. The use of EQs helps those who need guidance to develop lines of intellectual pursuit while also benefiting those who will later develop ideas and questions of their own as they create projects that go far beyond content introduced by the teacher.

Generating EQs can be a fraught part of curriculum design. My experience is that the framing EQs for a unit are most effective if I create them as part of my planning process as I research, evaluate sources, and craft project descriptions. I continue to revise the questions on my planning doc as I choose resources and create a learning plan with a trajectory to match the path of inquiry. If the questions are too narrow or simplistic there is a risk of inadvertently limiting interest or curiosity in the topic (McTighe & Wiggins, 2013). Phrasing questions in the most effective way is laborious as I attempt to become well-versed enough in the unit content that I understand areas of tension and debate among scholars.

Because the EQs are teacher-generated I make sure the unit includes many opportunities for students to contribute ideas and additional questions to the inquiry. In addition, students direct the part of their inquiry when they choose the focus for the projects they will create.

Below are some sample Essential Questions from different units I designed:

From a Unit on Violence, Militarism, and Alternatives

In what different ways is militarism ingrained in our society?

From a Unit on Identity and Belonging

How does society construct or destroy feelings of identity and belonging?

From a Unit on Revolutions

How does social change evolve?

From a Unit on early U.S. History

Who gets remembered?

Project-Based Learning

Although the term "project-based learning" seems to have been co-opted as an education buzzword with diluted meaning, it is true that when learning integrates real-world student discovery and creation, the roles of students and teachers are transformed in ways that benefit all. This reshaping of classrooms and knowledge helps students develop a sense of agency as learners and as people. If teachers maintain antiquated notions of students as information recipients, teaching and learning become a pointless game where, instead of connection and engagement, the main challenge for students is to read the teacher's mind while producing a product in which they don't feel invested.

The Coalition of Essential Schools developed the metaphor of students as workers, with teachers as mentors or coaches (CES Common Principles, n.d.). My time as a project-based teacher has helped me to investigate this metaphor and expand upon it. With the goal of designing learning that challenges students intellectually and creatively, I think of my students as creators. In order to support acts of creation, I shift among multiple roles as I frame the learning, design inquiry-based units, help students generate ideas, provide models of work, consult with students, give feedback on rough work, and structure experiences so that there is an audience for student projects.

This book contains many examples of projects my students created. These projects are not tacked on at the end of units or something that exists side by side with more traditional assessments. The projects are a way to immerse students in intellectual and creative work. They require students to build on the shared inquiry of the class by producing work that involves additional research, choice, and project design. Being asked to create in complex, sophisticated ways is inherently stimulating and creative. The more that students can be the ones *doing*, the more they are challenged to go beyond what they already know. Of course, merely completing teacher-designed assignments does not guarantee transformation or growth. Projects can be designed to enable students to go beyond ideas expressed in class, nurturing and supporting different forms of thought and creativity. (A selection of project examples can be found in Appendix section A.)

Shifting the work of school to investigation and creation provides opportunities for intellectual work to also be creative work. Creative expression through multiple modalities allows students to delve more deeply and viscerally into big ideas and discover new ways of thinking and being, and helps them undermine the false compartmentalization of different subjects that exists within academia. These creative opportunities allow students to find and develop unaccessed or unknown voices and skills.

In a unit on literary theory, students create a piece of artwork that demonstrates the ways they can view one text through multiple lenses, resulting in paintings, videos, songs, and poetry. The accompanying written analysis reveals multiple layers of understanding. In a poetry unit, students are surprised by the task of having to quickly prepare and then stage a performance of a poem they received at the beginning of the class period. Groups practice on their feet, finding different ways to embody the ideas within several Langston Hughes poems referencing dreams, knowing their peers are doing the same and that there will be a supportive audience when the performances take place toward the end of class. In a U.S. History class, study of the history of public education culminates with the creation of digital stories in which pairs of students decide their question for investigation and create a 2- to 3-minute video of still images, text, and narration designed to educate the public about aspects of the history of schools in the United States.

These kinds of learning are messy and complicated. My most fulfilling teaching days are filled with overlapping student voices, surprise, and opportunity. As I circulate around the room, I speak with young people who are grappling with challenges, generating and then revising ideas, and finding their way through the multiple stages of project creation. Depending on the day, my students may be sprawled out on the floor in groups, sitting individually as they stare down at their work on a screen, in quiet spaces editing video or audio, or clumped together in small reading huddles.

On some days, making work complex and real for my students means that their learning does not happen in my room and may not happen in my presence. They may be interviewing recent immigrants at a local nonprofit as part of an immigration oral history project, leaving school with a note from me to be at an appointment they set up at the beginning of a unit. They may be leaving our building to photograph or record video for a Field Note after having completed the text portion of the assignment. Or maybe all of us leave together to attend a workshop with a local dance company about the creation of site-specific art. These different experiences complicate what it means to be in school while shifting the experience of students to one of exploration and authentic creation.

When classes focus on ideas of creation, change, and agency, students are encouraged to explore their lived realities and beyond. These types of learning help young people examine the flawed world we know while moving toward creating the world of our dreams. Giving students permission and encouragement to do this work leads to engagement and empowerment of young people while giving them opportunities to do real, necessary work. Cocreating these experiences helps students understand themselves, their potential as intellectuals, their power as agents in the world, and their connection to communities.

Establishing Audiences for Student Work

A final strategy that helps make work complex and real is to create it for a larger audience and not solely for the teacher. Excerpts of papers may be read aloud as we sit in a large circle, project links may be posted to an online forum where we all offer feedback, or the work may be shared with an outside audience or be part of a project with outside collabora-tors. Whenever possible I have students create work that relates to real world scenarios and will be seen by others, not just me.

Even at times when an outside audience is not available, I construct a scenario that adds to the work. In a World History unit, students created a proposal for a museum exhibit that would convey their un-derstanding of colonialism to a wider audience. Students were told that they were speaking to a museum board of directors. The audience (their classmates) asked rigorous questions and filled out an evaluation form for each presentation as they prepared to vote on which exhibit should be funded by the museum. Providing students with this kind of simu-lated real-life context for their work helps them understand that their work has broader application and meaning. It also motivates them to be thorough and polished in their presentations.

PRIORITIZING STUDENT VOICES, DECENTRALIZING THE CLASSROOM

In our society, it is widely believed that because young people lack expe-rience, they aren't smart, capable, or insightful. These beliefs are often referred to as young people's oppression or adultism. In reality, young people see the world differently and are able to recognize injustice and question dominant paradigms, make intellectual connections, and take action in ways that adults often will not. Paolo Freire explained that learning to read the world and discovering the power of one's own voice are transformative experiences (Freire, 1983). Designing learning that prioritizes student voices also benefits the teacher, who can leave the position of authority in the front of the room and be side by side with students as they transform themselves through their work.

School matters to students when they are given opportunities to en-gage with the world around them and ask questions about issues that are often ignored or overlooked. As students engage by reflecting on their experiences, learning about our society, and both envisioning and work-ing for social change, they learn that there is substance to their ideas and that they can inhabit multiple roles in the world. When learning is de-signed in ways that prioritize student voices and thought, there is a clear pathway for students to invest themselves fully and genuinely in quality work that matters. Another way to think of this is to allow students to make meaning of content on their own terms.

In addition to regularly sharing both rough work and finished products out loud, students can generate questions and facilitate. When I prepare students well and successfully set them up to develop their own ideas, my students facilitate their own discussions by quoting sources, calling on each other, and questioning each other deeply. During these times I remind students to speak to each other and not solely to me. I position myself off to the side or behind other students, in order to make sure students speak to each other and shift away from a model where the teacher is always the center of the action.

Facilitating group class discussion can be a revolving classroom role, or classes can develop guidelines and systems for collectively run discussions. (An example would be having each speaker call on the next person to speak.) Classes can self-evaluate their performance and learn more about discussion and facilitation skills in the process. These are not moments when the teacher is invisible but rather when the role of the teacher is that of an assistant or guide who is ready to step in when needed before returning to the periphery.

My work, and I believe the work of schools, is to create more opportunities for students to connect with content and produce work that they feel they own. Rather than submit to something that is based on a distant administrator or outside authority's priorities, students should have opportunities to create work that allows them to investigate issues that they regard as meaningful. It is not that project criteria should be forgotten, but rather that we should design learning to provide students with choices as well as generative opportunities and possibilities. It is not enough to expose students to information; deep learning happens when we make space for students to do creative, challenging work in response to meaningful content. While that learning is happening, students should have multiple opportunities to explore and articulate their thoughts and discoveries.

Balancing Structure and Choice

One pathway that allows the role of students to shift away from passivity is through strategic and meaningful student choice. Too much structure can remove individual investment and creativity. On the other hand, when choice is not backed up with clear modeling of expectations and guidelines, many are left unsure of how to proceed. There are times when students are able to pursue their passions and independently create projects, and other times when students can be given choice in smaller, yet still significant, ways. The parameters of choice vary depending on the cycles of the school year, the students, the project, and other factors. For example, early in the school year or in the beginning stages of a unit when I want to establish shared reference points or knowledge, choice will be more limited. As the year or a unit progresses, I will create more opportunities for students to branch out and direct their own intellectual process. This continual dance involves providing enough structure while also enabling meaningful student choice for learners to find passion, voice, and sometimes even revelation through their work.

Most of the units I design begin with the whole class reading, writing, and discussing the same topics, but there is almost always a point where students are given opportunities to continue their investigation by creating a project on a related topic of their choosing. This means that many students will struggle to find a topic, angle, or approach that works for them. I support this authentic process of struggle while challenging them to create projects that present ideas that are unique and compelling. This means that I expect my students to do hard intellectual and creative work in order to succeed. I tell them that I want projects to be "professional quality" and ready for an outside audience. This means that students will have to revise well past what their teenage patience generally allows.

Balancing structure and choice is an aspect of curriculum design and classroom practice that requires regular attention and adjustment. Early in a unit I provide models and share carefully selected outside sources. The models and resources I select are intended not to establish narrow parameters of acceptable work but to establish norms for quality work. The goal is to inspire new ideas for students of what is possible while we begin a conversation about different potential approaches to the work. Once we have moved past the initial framing of the inquiry of a unit, students shift to designing their projects. In this stage I try to flood them with resources that will help them generate ideas, research more deeply, and produce work in innovative ways. We may read and analyze a mentor text as a class, or I will provide students with a detailed project guide that usually includes a source bank of links with a range of ideas and perspectives on the topic of the unit.

Design Your Own Learning Projects

I am continually trying to develop new strategies for students to own their work and produce creations that matter to them. One is to base part of a course on projects designed by the students themselves. With the criteria for these projects I provide an open door for exploration and discovery while sparking interest and possibility.

Several years ago, starting with the idea that projects should focus on "untold stories" or "hidden realities," I presented students with a range of sources, potential projects ideas, and models of work from journalists and previous students. They then had several days until their initial proposals were due for their Design Your Own Learning projects. Some students chose to work on their own while others self-selected into groups. I explained that the scale of the work needed to reflect the number of people working on the project. Proposals included four parts:

1. Question for investigation and goal of your project.
2. Research: How will you learn about your topic? What different models do you have for your work? (Must include at least four annotated sources.)
3. Process: How will you go about creating your product?
4. What is the final product? Who will see it? How will it influence people?

Once the proposals were submitted I began conferencing with students and groups, helping them modify and focus their initial ideas. At the beginning of each class session I asked some people to share their ideas with the whole class, knowing that other groups would benefit from hearing about the project ideas being developed. Students began to map out their goals for each week we would spend on the project. One group of three young women began by reading and writing dialogue journals in response to the book *On the Run: Fugitive Life in an American City* (Goffman, 2015). They were drawn in by the ethnography and the ways it described many of the dynamics they witnessed in their own neighborhoods, but 2 weeks into the work they still didn't have a clear idea for their final product. At the proposal stage I accepted their lack of larger vision as necessary for the development of a future compelling idea—many people don't know what they want to create until they have done some research and begun the design process itself.

When we were further into the process I reassured them, but also tried to nudge them toward something specific and compelling. "What different ideas or topics from the book are drawing your attention? Be specific. I'll come back in 15 minutes to see your list." I walked toward another group knowing that their annoyance with me was growing and that at this point they were not invested in the process that lay ahead. I also knew that much of what they were going through was a natural part of the struggle of having the responsibility to develop an idea and design work on their own and wanted to give them time on their own to move toward the next stage.

When I returned, after checking in with other student groups, they had the beginning of an idea. "We want to make a documentary about dark skinned versus light skinned," said Imani. "They mention it in the book and it's all around [us]." Each of the young women (all of whom were African American) had examples of why this issue mattered and how it impacted their lives and the lives of people they knew. Maybe most importantly, I was hearing them speak about it with clear interest and a desire to educate others. I asked them to tell me more as I recorded additional bullet points of ideas and questions on their project doc.

As I listened to them, I also shared some resources and ideas of my own. I let them know that some people refer to this issue of prejudice based on skin tone within the African American community as *colorism*. I recommended a documentary I knew that touched on issues of colorism. Joie knew of another documentary that she had watched on her own. I gave them several search terms to use for additional research and, after a moment of reflection, affirmed their idea of using social media posts as part of their research. Together we began the early process of outlining the different steps of a project on the issue that could be created for a wider audience. I was careful to position myself not as an expert on colorism but as a collaborator with their research. I affirmed their documentary idea but told them that to meet project requirements for a group of three (most groups in the room were groups of two), they would also have to create a substantial written component for their project that could live on a website side by side with the film they would make.

Four weeks later the young women were wrapping up the final stages of the documentary and website *For the Love of Black Girls* (lovecoloredgirls.weebly.com). I sat with each of them, reading through what they had written, offering ideas to polish the text. I pointed out some repeated grammar errors that I was observing and shared general ideas for strengthening the writing. After these individual check-ins I spoke with them as a group, asking them to further describe their plan for their multimedia component, taking the opportunity to ask them clarifying questions about their approach and pointing out decisions they would have to make during the video editing process.

They had divided the work among themselves. I eavesdropped from the other side of the room as they held each other accountable, sometimes hearing them express annoyance that someone had not completed a task assigned to them. They had interviewed multiple students during their lunch period and the video clips that they showed me were impressive. In one clip a young man speaks about his desire to date only light skinned girls. In another a darker skinned girl speaks about being continuously judged based on her skin color. In one of the posts on the site, Joie wrote, "As a young African American woman of a deeper skin tone, I constantly battle with the way I look on the outside," she wrote. "I always have been judged by the opposite sex because my hair is not a certain length and my skin is not close to white." The three students were in the final stages of a project they clearly cared deeply about, but they were also struggling with the reality of the amount of work required to produce something that they could feel proud of and share widely.

In the days after the project was completed and posted to the web (tinyurl.com/tfald6), the young women and I shared it through our social media accounts. It seemed to speak to an issue that mattered to many people; the number of views of the video and of posts and comments on social media continued to grow. The students (and I) were giddy as we watched the project spread well beyond what we had anticipated. Each day they reported the new numbers to me. When I told them I had been contacted by a journalist who wanted to write an article about their work, they stood in front of me with their eyes wide open, alternately hugging each other with excitement and expressing disbelief. In their interview, the students described their process, affirming the passion they felt for the topic and different ways they had both struggled and succeeded during the process. According to Joie, "It feels good when a teacher supports you about what you're passionate about instead of just saying, 'Follow my rules. Answer my questions'" (Dwyer, 2016).

Reflection and Flexibility

In *Pedagogy of the Oppressed* (2005), Paolo Freire discusses reflection as an essential part of learning and of becoming an agent of change in the world: "Within the word we find two dimensions, reflection and action, in such radical interaction that if one is sacrificed—even in part—the other immediately suffers" (p. 87). Understanding the interplay between reflection and action becomes even more important when we understand that school is not structured in a way that easily accommodates ambiguity and differentiation, both of which are necessary for reflection to occur. While this presents a challenge, the strategic integration of meaningful closings and reflection into classroom practice gives students multiple avenues for engaging with complex ideas and allows more students to find broader meaning in their work. Additionally, these activities help teachers to more deeply understand and adapt to the intellectual processes of our students.

I make the end of classes a time when students can deepen their own understandings and entire groups can share ideas and make meaning of content. These last moments, which usually occur after ideas have had a chance to marinate, can be when quiet thinkers finally articulate their ideas and move toward Freire's idea of *concientización* (which loosely translates as the development of awareness) (2005). At these times students can share final thoughts or lingering questions. Sometimes groups huddle together to generate these final class contributions. Additionally, when a large piece of work is submitted there are important opportunities for students to articulate their own learning and self-evaluate in order to improve learning and the quality of their work for the future. Often I have students complete a small assignment at the time of submission, answering questions such as:

1. What are the parts of the project that make you most proud? Why?
2. What are the parts that could be improved? How would you improve them?
3. If you were to do this project again, what would you do differently?

It is helpful for me to read these reflective assignments alongside the work that was submitted. More importantly, these examples of metacognition change students' relationships to content and the experience of being a student.

Recently, we spent a chunk of one of my World History classes discussing an excerpt from *The Power of Myth*, a conversation that Joseph Campbell had with Bill Moyers about enduring myths and the human condition (Campbell & Moyers, 1988). The students read an excerpt of the text during the previous class and had done a writing exercise that helped them begin to explore some of the ideas contained in the dialogue.

The discussion was interesting but felt aimless. Some students were interested in the idea of learning deeper messages by reading the myths of others. Others were struck by Campbell's idea that we are all imperfect. For many, it was unclear if they found anything of meaning in the reading. The body language in the classroom symbolized the lackluster moment. A few students turned to face whoever was speaking and eagerly responded, often referring to the text in front of them. Others were slouched in their chairs, rarely looking at the text or people who were speaking. Students knew that this was the beginning of our religion unit and had spent time earlier in the week attempting to create a definition of religion, yet if felt as if no one knew how to put these different pieces together successfully or effectively into larger, coherent ideas with greater meaning. I felt unsure about our status in this early part of our unit.

As the discussion slowed down and the clock approached the end of the period, I asked everyone to jot down a one-sentence final thought. After 2 silent minutes, we started in one corner of the room and quickly whipped around as, one after another, students shared final thoughts from the reading and discussion. It immediately became clear that a lot more deep and rich thinking had happened than I had realized. "Religions are glorified myths," said a student who had been quiet all period. "We all need ways to find meaning in our lives," offered a young man who had previously seemed to find very little meaning in the discussion. Incorporating a brief activity of reflection and sharing appeared to have advanced student thinking and changed my understanding of the lesson along with our status moving forward in the unit.

A final element of decentralized, student-centered classrooms is the need for adaptive and flexible teachers. At times it becomes painfully clear that my curriculum or lesson design could be adapted to better suit more learners. I see that students haven't understood my instructions, I failed to clearly explain the connection between different parts of a unit, or my expectations for what students can accomplish are unrealistic. Often these suggestions for changes come from the students themselves. In these scenarios, I aim to let go of my ego, quickly adapt, accept new ideas, and allow students to proceed with their work in a way that is engaging and meaningful to them.

The Struggle of Creation

Some of what I now consider my most successful teaching experiences began as an exercise in frustration. I was working with 12th-graders who were designing their own learning in their English class. As described earlier, my goal was to have clear requirements but also a large amount of choice and a requirement for self-directed learning and creation. (See Appendix section D for Design Your Own Learning project description.)

Every time I sat down with Amanda for an update on her work, she had little progress to show me. She was stuck and I didn't understand what was happening. I knew Amanda was capable and motivated, but she was not making progress on this project. "Can you show me your latest draft?" I asked as I sat down next to her, hoping that something had changed since I spoke with her days ago.

"I don't know if my idea is good. And I'm not really sure I want to tell this story." Looking at her screen I could see that her document had very little on it. I was puzzled; she had told me she completed a chunk of the writing for the script and I didn't know her as someone who was dishonest. I tried to swallow my frustration, and sat down with her, knowing there were also several other students needing me to check in with them. "What's going on, Amanda? It seemed like you had an interesting idea and you had a good start, but now you have nothing." I was careful to try and strike a supportive tone while also making it clear that she was falling behind with the checkpoints and work necessary for the project. Amanda began to tell me about the incidents she wanted to write about, a time when she had been bullied and responded by becoming a bully herself. She had written a draft but then erased it all. She explained that she was scared about telling this story and unsure of how others would react. I reassured her of the value of the story and the importance of sharing it with others, hoping that my interest and excitement would encourage her to move forward with the work.

Together, we mapped out a plan: She would write the script, revise, and then record it as a radio piece to be shared with others. As we talked I took notes on the ideas and necessary steps for completion on her Google Doc, making sure she would have access to the substance of our conversation when she got home. We agreed that she wouldn't call out those that bullied her but would reveal what it was like to be in this situation and how easy it had been for her to switch from the one under attack to the one targeting others.

There were many more bumps in the road, but developing a vision and exposing Amanda to models of similar work got her excited and gave her a structure for her own work. Weeks later, at the end of the process, she offered some reflections:

The work I've been producing has been extremely personal. While I write these stories for an audience, I think it's important to acknowledge that I've been writing these stories for myself. I've known these stories for years, but it's a relief to finally sit down and get a chance to put my thoughts on paper. It's therapeutic to me to publicize these personal stories. If school consisted of teachers lecturing the class, I would not enjoy going to school every day. . . . The opportunities made me go outside my comfort zone and gave me a head start in the right direction to fulfill my dreams of becoming a journalist.

Amanda's final radio piece on bullying was profound and insightful (tinyurl.com/tfald18). Because she brought a unique voice to a current issue, I shared the work with a collaborator of ours who works in radio and it was broadcast by our local NPR station. The whole class enthusiastically celebrated the power of what she created and her success. Of course, not all students were able to create work that was broadcast to a wider audience and not all final products were as impressive as Amanda's. What was universal was an opportunity for students to create work they designed, where the teacher was present as a rigorous yet supportive consultant, as the elevation of student voices became the focus. The result was a shift in the meaning of and experience of school.

CODA

Students will not invest themselves in complex intellectual work unless they feel that their voices matter in the classroom. Any community that asks people to learn and be vulnerable must be a place where people know that they can be honest and that they will be heard. One of the clearest ways this is communicated is when teachers are tuned in to and looking to learn from students, changing the dynamics of what it means to teach and what it means to learn.

I have come to understand school as a place of potential where my role is to show students to a path of inquiry and creation. I am present throughout the process, inhabiting multiple roles, waiting at various places along the path, offering support, critique, and guidance. It has been humbling to realize that, at times, once the stage has been set for students to create the work, my most important task is to get out of the way!

These types of learning challenge students to question, reflect, examine, and analyze, a process that can lead students to create work that goes beyond their expectations of their own abilities. The result is an experience of school that changes students' understandings of their potential in the world and reveals a universal truth from Walt Whitman's "Song of Myself" (1855/2005):

"I am large, I contain multitudes."

CHAPTER 4

Envisioning New Roles for Teachers

I did not want to raise you in fear or false memory. I did not want you forced to mask your joys and bind your eyes. What I wanted for you was to grow into consciousness.

—Ta-Nehisi Coates (2017)

Frequently, when visitors enter my classroom, they have trouble finding me. This is not because I look particularly young but because most of the time that my classes are in session I am seated with students or squatting next to tables, taking time to check in or confer about work in progress. This was true recently as students were peer-reviewing drafts for Advanced Essays they were writing:

> I pull up a chair and join a group of students at their table. They are leaving feedback on each other's docs, typing notes about writing that works well along with questions to guide revision. Earlier in the year we discussed feedback and modeled effective comments for the class before I introduced students to the framework they are now using.
>
> "What type of feedback would be most helpful?" I ask as I squat down, knowing that if I want to check in with every student, I have only a couple of minutes for each conversation. Some students respond with specific ideas while others provide me little direction at the beginning of our conversations. I am a bit like a detective trying to quickly determine the status and needs of different individuals. Sitting next to Jasmin, I lean over to see her screen and quickly scan what she's written while trying to figure out what I can offer to help her move her work forward. "These are really powerful ideas that you're beginning to investigate," I

tell her, intentionally beginning our conference with an affirmation. "I wonder how you can strengthen the question that frames your paper? Also, the descriptive scene is interesting, but it isn't yet clear how it relates to your investigation. Can you think of a way to make it clearer?"

When I'm sitting next to Reggie, the conversation has a different focus. "I'm trying to understand what you're writing about. The first part of your paper seems to focus on the idea of economic inequality, but then it shifts to information about family. How are these connected?"

With Kenny, our short conversation becomes a strategy session for him as an English-language learner. "I've noticed that you regularly struggle with verb tenses in English. What do you need to do in order to submit a paper that doesn't have verb tense mistakes? How can I, and others, help?"

REFRAMING TEACHER VOICE

The above vignette describes writing conferences, but also encapsulates much more. These small conversations would not be possible without a reframing of the traditional idea of teacher voice. Instead of an all-knowing expert who is telling students what they need to do or what they need to know, I position myself as a humble, inquisitive consultant who comes to the students in order to help them further develop their ideas as they produce work that will be compelling for a wider audience. My conversations with students are intellectual, often helping them explore connections between emerging thinking and sources or probing while also encouraging, seeking to clarify language and ideas. While these short check-ins almost always feel rushed, they are essential moments of interpersonal connection between me and students. They allow me to validate students' work and intellect while offering strategic ideas to move their work along in ways that will improve the final products.

While one stereotype of the desired voice for teachers is stern, commanding, and uncompromising, the reality of teaching entails more complexity and nuance. Power and authority are an inherent part of the teacher's role, but student respect and engagement do not develop from threats or a stern tone. Effective teacher voice uses a combination of flexibility and firmness while keenly reading individuals and the pulse of a group in order to find the best approach for progress. By intentionally limiting our power and influence teachers create participatory learning environments where student ideas are centered. Teachers have captive audiences, but we must remember that some of the most important work involves making space for students to share ideas, respond to each other, and direct the learning.

To teach in this way means maintaining an acute awareness of the power of one's own voice in the classroom. It is an inquiry stance that helps teachers maintain a critical awareness of their roles as classroom leaders (Cochran-Smith & Lytle, 2009). Assuming this stance means a "move from relationships based on power over other people to relationships based on shared power" (Spirit in Action, 2010). In order to reframe teacher voice and for a power shift to occur, teachers must continually seek to know their students deeply while working to develop trusting, supportive relationships.

In addition to rethinking teacher voice, this chapter explores other roles teachers can inhabit. These ways of supporting students and structuring learning are fluid and, because they are connected, frequently overlap. My hope is that envisioning the roles separately will help teachers to inhabit multiple positions fully while also understanding ways the need for these roles can manifest one after another or even concurrently. Utilizing multiple roles allows teachers to change the framework of school learning, leading toward the idea of a living democracy. The roles I find most important are facilitator, collaborator, and consultant-scholar.

TEACHERS AS FACILITATORS

Those who successfully facilitate in learning spaces help groups to function in ways that support individual growth. The life and dynamics of the whole group are intertwined with the experiences of individuals. Teacher facilitation includes designing learning activities, deciding different formats for learning or discussions (whole class or small groups), and developing supports for students when they struggle.

Comments and feedback from students are invaluable for teachers looking to successfully facilitate learning. Sometimes these insights arise from unplanned interactions or observations (also known as eavesdropping!), and at other times activities can be structured so that students share insights about their own learning. By stepping back and taking time to observe, teachers notice things about engagement, group dynamics, and individuals that are easy to miss when they are actively leading class.

By listening and observing, teachers are able to develop insights that assist in the planning and facilitation of future lessons. This knowledge allows teachers to speak meaningfully with students about their work and learning. I recently listened in on a student speaking to a friend. His comment changed my perception of him as a learner. "I wish I could do this semester over," he said with remorse. This student, whom I'll call James, had frequently frustrated me with his behavior. Every time I spoke with him about his work, it was clear that he was engaged and intellectually capable of producing high-quality products, yet whenever I gave students time to work, he spent that time talking to friends or looking at websites that had no connection to impending deadlines.

James's comment and his tone of despair helped me begin to see him as someone interested in doing well in class. I realized that the behaviors I was observing represented his current inability to regularly make choices that reflected his long-term values and desires. When I began to understand his struggles my frustration turned into sympathy. Instead of approaching him with exasperation, I became more of an ally, made the choice to limit my frustration, and approached him with the goals of assisting him to focus, succeed, and be a positive contributor to the larger classroom community. Together we created a "to do" task list that he and I could reference every time I conferenced with him. I regularly let him know that I was going to call on him to share ideas or examples in upcoming whole-class discussions, hoping these successful contributions would motivate him to complete more written work.

Nonviolence trainer George Lakey introduced me to the idea that facilitators create a container, or "a social order that supports safety" for a group (2010, p. 14). These containers make it possible to explore ideas and take risks. Strong containers are products of clearly developed norms and thoughtful, supportive facilitation. Students should feel free to share thoughts and ideas honestly and must be regularly reminded of the expectation and behaviors for listening deeply and openly to their peers. These behavioral nudges from teachers can come before an activity when instructions include information about expectations and norms. At other times expectations can be communicated to individuals or smaller groups during classroom conferencing or check-in times.

Strong containers allow students to feel safe and respected while encouraging them to take risks and bring their authentic selves to the learning process. I often remind my students to explain their disagreement with someone's thinking or ideas rather than looking to start an argument. At times this is a difficult distinction, yet students and classroom dynamics benefit from a framework that welcomes multiple perspectives and encourages discourse while discouraging interpersonal conflicts.

Teacher-facilitators also work to decentralize knowledge. They structure activities in ways that truly value student insight and thinking, shifting the way ideas are positioned. The structures press students to use evidence in order to speak in informed ways about the topic and the inquiry. They are expected to create ideas and insights rather than waiting for them to come from those seen as experts.

Teachers who facilitate peer feedback allow students to take ownership over the intellectual components of an assignment. A classroom where the teacher is the only legitimate source for feedback or ideas quickly becomes a frustrating place for all. If I were the only one responding to student work, many learning opportunities would be missed. By giving and receiving feedback from others, students further develop metacognitive skills (awareness of their own intellectual processes) and insights about their work, allowing them to expand their thinking as they define their own areas for growth and improvement. (See Appendix section C for examples of Self-Evaluation/Peer Review forms.)

When students review each other's work, the teacher is able to move around the room and add to a process that is already underway. In the opening vignette of this chapter, I was willing to look at students' work only after it had been reviewed by two peers, thereby elevating the importance of the peer reviews and insuring that students had received some feedback before I got to them. Before offering my own comments I quickly scanned the feedback from others, using it to inform the conversation about revision.

Another important aspect of teachers as facilitators is cultural work. One way to envision this work is articulated by Henry Giroux: "In this perspective, culture is not viewed as monolithic or unchanging, but as a shifting sphere of multiple heterogeneous borders where different histories, languages, experiences, and voices intermingle amid diverse relations of power and privilege" (2005, p. 32). In a classroom this means approaching individuals, groups, and content with an attitude of learning and investigation. Many of my students grow up in neighborhoods, families, and cultures vastly different from my own experience. By first acknowledging this, creating the space for honest communication, and listening deeply, I help my students understand that while my life may be outside of their circles of familiarity, I am curious to learn about their knowledge and understandings. Cultural workers know that it is possible to connect across cultural divides but assumptions about beliefs, values, and experience are often inaccurate. As with any scenario, if my initial assumption is that I know the reality, experiences, or beliefs of my students and don't need to hear their ideas or bear witness to their truths, trust is broken.

By working to bring what is marginalized in our society into the mainstream of the classroom, teacher-facilitators can make their classes liberating spaces where students develop new ideas and consciousness about themselves and their world. It is impossible to design transgressive learning experiences or teach reflectively without a clear understanding of the social construction of identity. Some of my own knowledge of self is that mainstream U.S. society treats whiteness as normal, a default setting. I am also aware that having grown up identified as male strongly influences my perception of the world. Understanding my own personal and family history, acknowledging my own power, rank, and privilege, and recognizing the dynamics of white supremacy, patriarchy, and identity in the United States all help me to create a climate where honest connections can be made across cultural divides (McIntosh, 2003; Rankine, 2019). Intentionally working to develop this kind of self-understanding is essential if I want to design curriculum that speaks to multiple experiences.

Teacher-facilitators who are cultural workers also understand that conflict is an inevitable part of real-world work. In *Sitting in the Fire*, Arnold Mindell writes that "engaging in heated conflict instead of running away from it is one of the best ways to resolve the divisiveness that prevails on every level of society" (2014, p. 12). For teachers, this means establishing, modeling, and maintaining classroom norms that allow students to discuss controversial issues, mediating an argument, or designing curriculum that is intended to challenge students' worldviews.

Mindell's work dissects group dynamics and demonstrates the potential for large-group transformation. He reminds facilitators to pay attention to power, rank, and the mainstream and the margins of each group, to acknowledge those margins, and to create opportunities for the mainstream to hear from them. In classrooms, this can happen through carefully designed activities and strategic facilitation. One example is to ask for "different opinions" or "other perspectives" in order to provide openings for students who have not voiced their ideas.

Part of the beauty of what happens when teachers become facilitators is that youth rise and become agents in their own education and in their own lives. Instead of waiting for others to advise them and make decisions for them, they empower themselves to inquire, converse, and create in ways that often inspire.

TEACHERS AS LEAD COLLABORATORS

There are times when I am shocked into recognition about how much I ask of my students. While much of my school career was spent behind a desk receiving information, I require my students to actively create. At times I ask them to inhabit new roles that they have not chosen by presenting in front of their peers, speaking to groups of adults, or exploring new possibilities of how to be in the world, yet they regularly rise to the occasion. None of this would be possible if they didn't feel that others in the classroom community and I were supporting them. Part of what makes this possible is my positioning as lead collaborator, in which I plan classes so that whole-group activities model collaborative practices. I then ask students to emulate what they saw and experienced.

A key element of the practice of teachers who play the role of lead collaborators is the use of multiple forms of modeling. When I introduce a project, I use models to demonstrate form and spark students' thinking and imaginations. Recently, when I asked students to write text and then create multimedia that accompanied the writing, I showed them "Invisible Child" (Elliott, 2013), a journalism piece that uses multiple forms of storytelling to investigate the life of a homeless girl in New York City. Once students had a sense of the form and the concept I was proposing, we spent time collaboratively generating topics for their projects. I will often have students make an initial list of their own or work in small groups. Then the ideas are shared out loud as I or a student scribe collects them in a doc that everyone can access. In these moments I will take time to workshop ideas out loud with the class, illustrating ways to deepen their thinking, helping them develop pathways for making their work more complex. The combination of modeling, collective brainstorming, and my feedback provides students with both a wide range of possibilities and clear pathways for success.

Teacher-collaborators often mentor others as they pursue inquiry. Knowing that deep, meaningful learning happens when people have the experience of discovery, not when they are told what to think, I carefully construct my responses when students ask me for my opinion or my personal analysis of an issue. It is tempting to immediately respond with my own ideas. Instead, I restrain myself and respond with questions that push the thinking of my students toward new places. At other times, it is clear that a student needs a model or a starting point in order to proceed on their own.

In addition to using professional work in the world as models, I try to seize every opportunity to highlight quality student work as a guide for others. These whole-class moments of support are shout-outs or mini-celebrations that nurture a collaborative ethos and provide opportunities to analyze form and effective strategies or techniques. This may happen by putting a student's work up on the screen and asking them to read it out loud to the class or handing out an excerpt of student work on paper. I ask students to notice specific details that make the work effective or powerful. After a list is generated I ask for questions for the author or creator, making sure students don't use this as an opportunity to criticize the work but rather push the author to consider additional ideas or strategies to inform their revisions.

One day, as students enter the room, I pull Jasmin aside and ask her if I can share a draft of her work with the class. When class begins I tell everyone, "I'd like to start out by giving a shout-out. Let's all give Jasmin a hand for writing an amazing rough draft." Students yell and applaud, happy to begin class with positive news and a chance to let loose. I project Jasmin's doc onto the screen and begin modeling:

> "Jasmin, can read your intro paragraph to the class?"
>
> After Jasmin stands and reads, I begin our process: "What did people like about this intro? What's working?" Several students respond. I encourage them to speak directly to Jasmin, providing specific details and appreciations for her work. I speak again after we've heard from multiple students: "Jasmin, I really like the way that you used a descriptive scene to draw readers right into the moment. The description you provided was detailed and poignant. I began to wonder about the issues of identity and social class which you then go on to investigate in your paper."

After the work has been celebrated and analyzed I ask students to turn a critical eye by providing feedback in a format that will help Jasmin:

> "What questions do you have for Jasmin that will help her improve her work? Jasmin, remember to just listen and take notes during

this part. As the author, you get to decide what feedback to integrate and what to ignore."

As mentioned previously, I intentionally ask for questions rather than criticisms or directives with the goal of providing the author with a range of possibilities for revision.

The above scene is an example of a lead collaborator generating discussion around a sample of student work in order to benefit the work of everyone in the room. By avoiding the stance of a potentially punitive authority figure and structuring the activity as one of noticing, acknowledgment, celebration, and supportive yet critical review, students experience a protocol and develop an understanding of the expectations for working in small groups with their peers. I structure the conversation in a way that works to eliminate judgment and allows the author to maintain artistic control of their work, to create a safe, supportive climate for students to honestly evaluate their own work and progress.

There are times when the role of lead collaborator entails individual, personalized attention to students who are struggling. Last year, one of my students hit a wall every time she began a writing assignment. She would sit, staring at her blank computer screen, getting more and more disconsolate as the people around her progressed with their work. The more I worked with this student, the more it became apparent that once she had a beginning, she could proceed with the rest of the work on her own. I began to check in with her in the early stages of projects and ask her about her ideas. Once I heard some of her early thoughts, I would offer sample opening sentences that I created on the spot. These small offerings often made it possible for her to find a way to proceed with the work.

It is liberating to abandon the idea that I'll assign work, students will rush to complete it without investing in the product, I'll grade it, and we'll move on to the next thing. Now I think of my role as showing students the beginning of a path that they must explore for themselves. They are the ones who figure out their direction and the shape of their final destination. I am present, as a collaborator, waiting at various places along the path, offering support, critique, and guidance.

TEACHERS AS CONSULTANTS AND SCHOLARS

Teachers who are consultants frame units of study and classroom practice around inquiry, using deep questions to help students develop the intellectual feistiness to question and investigate what many have learned to accept as given. These teacher consultants modify their approach to knowledge and information in accordance with people and situations. They provide access to information and ideas and help students make decisions on their own terms. Rather than assuming they know best, they ask, prod, validate, and connect ideas.

Consulting is most effective when it connects students with sources that help move their ideas forward and give them a clearer sense of what and how they can create. Teacher-consultants know that it is not enough to set students loose once a question or issue has been identified. In order to successfully frame inquiry, they need to be scholars, researching and gathering information, tapping personal networks, and learning from experts in various fields. With this access to information and ideas, they strategically design lessons and units. These teacher-consultant-scholars curate resources so that student research can be directed and efficient. Providing a range of quality sources as entry points for students allows students with different academic skills to proceed according to their strengths. Some will use the sources provided as background before they research on their own. Others, who may need more support, will use them as the bulk of the evidence for their own work.

One strategy for this curation of resources for students is for teachers to use social bookmarking. (An example of this is provided in Chapter 2 in the Modern-Day de Tocqueville project.) This tech tool allows teachers to continually collect resources that are organized by tags. When a class is working on a unit related to a theme, the teacher can share an entire curated collection of online sources with a single URL.

Functioning learning communities cannot be based on falsehoods or exclusion. Fresh, uninhibited perspectives that young people develop mean that they easily identify when curriculum does not have meaning to them or the world. Teacher-consultant-scholars identify diverse texts and create curriculums that function as what many educators speak of as both windows and mirrors for students (Sims Bishop, 1990, p. ix). A text is not inherently either a window or a mirror, but teachers can develop curriculum with the knowledge that chosen sources serve multiple functions for diverse grouping of students. Windows and mirrors can be utilized strategically for students from different backgrounds with the understanding that young people need and deserve access to both.

Windows expose us to the others' realities. For students who grow up in what many call the mainstream of this country and are conditioned to think of themselves and their lives as a default normal, windows provide necessary access to different realities and understandings of the world (Training for Change, 2018). These windows challenge students to question power structures and assumptions while developing insights about and understandings of the experiences of individuals from different social groups.

No one should grow up without mirrors, feeling that their experiences or voice are without value. For some young people in our society, most public representations of their lived realities are negative or lacking in complexity and substance. For these young people, learning that affirms the familiar while offering opportunities to develop a public voice and examine one's own story and history is crucial to developing feelings of belonging and agency. Teachers working to employ these pedagogies sustain "the lifeways of communities" and add to the "ongoing work of educational justice" (Paris, Alim, & Ferlazzo, 2017).

These understandings of windows and mirrors, and a practice that provides students with a broad assortment of each, are practices of culturally responsive and sustaining teaching that change emphasis and form depending on students' cultural contexts and communities (Paris & Alim, 2017). Students from a range of backgrounds must be presented with opportunities to "transcend the negative effects of the dominant culture" (Ladson-Billings, 2009, p. 19). While it is clear how this transcendence serves historically marginalized communities, these practices also provide an essential framework within communities where privilege abounds. Young people who grow up insulated from social issues greatly need to be exposed to different realities and challenged to see beyond "the white gaze," developing understandings of multiple perspectives and experiences (Morrison, 2013).

Within the practice of developing culturally responsive and sustaining curriculum, there is a danger of selecting content that consists solely of narratives of submission or suffering. To merely show how bad things are or were is not a pathway that leads to deep learning. Students need to understand issues, including stories of oppression and inequality, on complex levels. It is possible to do this while maintaining a lens that emphasizes stories of resistance, agency, and change. This humanizes people whose stories are often glossed over or misrepresented and allows learners to focus on complexity rather than simplistic narratives or "a single story" (Adichie, 2009). I attempt to demonstrate this stance of humanization in the multiple projects and student work samples integrated throughout the book. My efforts are enriched by conversations with other educators and by materials developed by professional teaching organizations and networks. Most frequently I find myself turning to Rethinking Schools, Teaching Tolerance, Educolor, Disrupt Texts, and others. A more complete list of teaching resources is available in Appendix section H.

A final role of the teacher-scholar-consultant is to make intellectual conversations with individual and small groups of students a core element of classroom practice. By leaving the front of the room, checking in, conversing and consulting with students, teachers shift the paradigm of what it means to create knowledge and upend beliefs about who is capable or qualified to do intellectual work. These conversations with students reveal classroom truths that would otherwise go unnoticed. For example, too often I find myself assuming that I know what a student is attempting to accomplish or articulate with their work, only to realize that I misunderstood.

These short conversations provide moments of insight and connection that can easily be missed. If I approach with questions that are too broad or fail to pick up on subtle signals from students, I fail as a consultant, and we may not connect in a way that gives me knowledge of a student's thought process. I try to make sure to position myself so I can see the student and the screen of their device as I sit or kneel at their level. After greeting students, I ask for specifics: "What have you done so far? What part are you working on now?" or "What is the most interesting source you've found? What are you struggling to find?" or "What main idea are you developing for your conclusion?" When I ask the right questions, my connections with even the most reticent students get stronger. By reminding myself to approach each student with the intent of listening and understanding, I strive to figure out their thinking before sharing my own ideas.

CODA

Those of us who spend our days with young people know that teaching is an enormous interpersonal challenge and that student motivation and progress are often tenuous. Students have few reasons to invest themselves in their work if they don't feel valued as individuals, as thinkers, and as creators. When teachers shift the roles they inhabit with students, they build relationships and get a more nuanced sense of student progress and understanding, which helps to nurture emerging student ideas. It is by facilitating, collaborating, and consulting with students that teachers help establish participatory, intellectual communities.

Grace Lee Boggs, activist, philosopher, and visionary, passed away in 2015 at the age of 100. Boggs was deeply inspired and informed by Martin Luther King Jr.'s idea of the beloved community. In *The Next American Revolution* (Boggs & Kurashige, 2012), she wrote:

> We urgently need to bring to our communities the limitless capacity to love, serve, and create for and with each other. We urgently need to bring the neighbor back into our hoods, not only in our inner cities but also in our suburbs, our gated communities, on Main Street and Wall Street, and on Ivy League campuses. (p. 44)

Our schools continue to struggle to move beyond a model of education where students' lived realities are regularly ignored. When teachers inhabit different roles and model what they value, students are more likely to experience school as a place of belonging and transformation. Love, serve, and create. Grace Lee Boggs couldn't have been more right.

CHAPTER 5

Decolonizing School

What are the words you do not yet have? What do you need to say? What are the tyrannies you swallow day by day and attempt to make your own, until you will sicken and die of them, still in silence?

. . . And of course I am afraid, because the transformation of silence into language and action is an act of self-revelation, and that always seems fraught with danger.

—Audre Lorde, 1998

For many students, the experience of school is a series of lessons about the necessity of submerging their primary identities and cultures in order to succeed academically. These students are repeatedly taught about "appropriate behavior" and told that the path through school, and society, is easier if one conforms to mainstream cultural standards.

Students need tools to navigate a range of spaces throughout their lives. Demanding that they conform to one standard serves to silence and negate aspects of their identities while setting the stage for endless struggles over compliance. Whether this happens by design or by default, the result is that many students experience school learning as something external to who they are and to what matters to them. In contrast, it is possible for teachers to create spaces and experiences for students that allow them to explore the complexities of power within society and multiple ways of expressing and embracing culture and individuality. This is what Carla Shalaby so beautifully describes as qualities of free people in her book *Troublemakers*: "A free person retains her power, her right to self-determination, her opportunity to flourish, her ability to love and be loved, and her capacity for hope" (2017, p. xv). These qualities, which are part of the essence of being human, should not be negotiated or denied within the walls of schools. Making space for all students to reclaim and sustain their identities is to decolonize school, detaching it from structures and practices that validate some while marginalizing others.

INSIGHTS FROM AOTEAROA, NEW ZEALAND

An opportunity I had to work with teachers in Aotearoa, New Zealand, helped push my understandings of the ways school learning can be designed to affirm one's identity. During my time overseas, which was the result of a Fulbright Award, I began to use both the Indigenous and the colonial names, as do many others, to emphasize the bicultural aspect of the country. In Aotearoa, New Zealand, there is legal acknowledgment that there is more than one dominant culture and that there are competing value systems, a reality that is also explicitly enacted in some schools.

Coming from the United States, I grew up attempting to make sense of the experience of living in a nation-state that is a product of colonial conquest. In Aotearoa, I was taken with the different, often public, ways that many people and the government grapple with their own colonial history, seeking to honor and make space for the indigenous Māori culture. While I immersed myself in the culture of New Zealand and spent extensive time in schools during the half school year I spent there, my observations were undoubtedly impacted by my status as an outsider and my bias toward certain types of information and knowledge.

There is extensive racism in New Zealand, and pressing social issues. At the same time, many people spoke of the need to address these issues and expressed a desire to build a more equitable society in ways I found inspiring. Small symbols, such as government signs that included indigenous Māori names alongside English names, meant that one's daily consciousness was challenged to recognize the complexity of different histories. In every school I visited, even if it was primarily White, there were examples of indigenous Māori art and language.

Early in my stay in Aotearoa, I was preparing a presentation for the faculty of a secondary school. I shared some of my ideas with my local mentors, seeking feedback and checking for cultural relevance. I was advised to prepare a *mihimihi* or a traditional Māori greeting to begin the presentation. I balked. Wouldn't it be disrespectful to butcher a language I don't know by pretending to speak it in front of a group? Why present myself in a way that entails co-opting another culture? I was reassured that this would be seen as honoring Māori culture and that making an attempt, even if it was not entirely successful, would be seen as respectful.

I began writing my *mihimihi*, learning from others how to place myself in context for the audience by describing the mountain I identify with, the body of water I identify with, the name of my hometown, and my name. Once again, I turned to mentors for advice, shocked to learn that not only did it make sense to begin a speech to a group in this way, it was supposed to be presented in a loud, booming voice!

The day of the presentation, I was introduced by the principal and stepped forward to begin:

> *Tēnā koutou, tēnā koutou, tēnā koutou katoa . . .*
> [Greetings, greetings, greetings all . . .]

The majority White, mostly non-Indigenous (*Pākehā* in Māori) teaching staff sat attentively, listening closely. I was in a situation where the rules had changed. The norms required the dominant culture to step back and prioritize an indigenous practice despite the fact that it was not necessarily within a zone of comfort for many in the room.

BICULTURALISM AND CREATING SPACE IN SCHOOLS

My experiences in New Zealand helped me to pay closer attention to what are often invisible structures within classrooms and schools. In *Coloring in the White Spaces: Reclaiming Cultural Identity in Whitestream Schools* (2017), Ann Milne, former principal of Kia Aroha College, a secondary school, documents different ways Māori students have been able to succeed as *themselves*. An important premise of Milne's work is that the structure of schools is not neutral; it is a product of colonial history. (These structures are what she illuminatingly names Whitestream.) This naming of what can often seem invisible or unchangeable provides us with an opportunity to examine and question its dominance. Part of the Māori Education Strategy, or *Ka Hikitia* (2013), published by the Ministry of Education, that Milne and her students successfully embody states the goal of helping "all Māori students gain the skills, qualifications, and knowledge they need to succeed and to be proud in knowing who they are as Māori." There is profound meaning to this idea of having students succeed in ways that allow them to reclaim and sustain, rather than relinquish, their cultural identities.

While school can be perceived as a universally valued experience, the reality is that students' ideas of important knowledge and values often differ greatly from the stated goals of school. Two New Zealand researchers offer a reminder about the roots of school practices: "What counts as school knowledge, the way school knowledge is organized, re-sourced, taught, and evaluated, the underlying codes that structure such knowledge . . . is determined by the dominant culture" (Tomlins-Jahnke & Durie, 2008). Students and families are often put in the situation of prioritizing either school values or home values; traditional structures can make merging the two impossible.

An emphasis on providing students from all backgrounds with op-portunities to reclaim and sustain their cultures and who they are shifts the experience of school. It makes learning less about fulfilling external requirements and more about investing in a process central to one's cur-rent and future identity. Focusing on personal and cultural affirmation along with academic success requires us to examine the structure and content of school. These understandings bring us to one of the most important, regularly unasked questions about schools: What should count as knowledge and education? Answering this question in ways that support students' lives and identities brings us closer to the goal of decolonizing school.

In a blog post about "white supremacy in our classrooms," Milne poses questions about decolonizing classrooms, encouraging teachers to dissect the often invisible layers of content and pedagogy: "Whose norms, values, and worldviews are implicit in this learning? Are others' norms, values, and worldviews left out?" (Milne, 2019; adapted from Morreira & Luckett, 2019). These insights and questions, along with my experiences of people overtly grappling with the legacies of colo-nialism in Aotearoa, New Zealand, helped me to understand that some of my classroom work has been an attempt to offer an embodiment of a decolonized space to my students. Rather than establish expecta-tions that mimic norms of the dominant culture, the work is intended to provide openings for student-directed investigation, encourage new and unique forms of expression, and open pathways to challenge power and domination in society. What follows are two examples of such attempts to create decolonized learning spaces, including examples of the student products that emerged.

THE RE-PLACE-ING PROJECT

Several years ago a friend mentioned a project at a local art space in our city. Not knowing if they would be interested in working with young people, I reached out, asking if my students could participate. I was enthusiastic in the early stages, but also cautious. Outside collaborations can result in extraordinary experiences for students but can also be fraught. I see no purpose in collaborating with groups and individuals that do not share an ethos of valuing student voices and creations. These ill-fated pairings can feel oppressive and trap students and teachers in unhealthy dynamics with outsiders. Collaborators must be willing to listen to students and avoid the attitude that students should act as passive receptacles of information. Young people are quick to sense condescension and will feel justifiably insulted by someone who does not respect their knowledge.

In this case, my sense was that there was a shared vision and that the collaboration would be a unique experience for students to have ownership over the process of creating work for a larger audience. What resulted was an opportunity for students to have their work published online (and for a select few, in an accompanying book), as part of a city-wide art project, alongside the work of professional artists. The structure of the Re-PLACE-ing project allowed students to create in a way that affirmed their interests, identities, and lived experiences.

The project began with a visit to the Painted Bride Art Center. After taking the subway across the city and walking through a neighborhood that was unfamiliar to many, students were enthusiastically greeted by Art Center staff. Students got a tour of the building and saw the current exhibits, providing them with examples and models of socially engaged art. Next, the students were seated in a section of the gallery, and the director and I made our pitch. Over the next 6 weeks, students were going to create digital Field Notes or creative, personal text and multimedia submissions, for the Re-PLACE-ing project. The goals of the project were to "build an expanded archive of cultural memory that includes multiple histories, re-place-ing the established with new narratives and understandings" (Re-PLACE-ing Philadelphia, n.d.). We explained the intent of "utiliz[ing] art-making as a lens for viewing the city and its history, examining the geography of Philadelphia and its complex histories as a basis for exploring relevant issues." As we spoke and shared examples of different Field Notes that had already been made, I saw some eyebrows raise and students glance at each other with expressions of mild interest but it seemed that most of this early positive energy was due to the fact that we were on a trip, not because they were yet sold on the work.

The next day in class I aimed to change this. After asking students about their impressions of the trip, I put a piece of paper on each table.

With the goals for the project up on the projector, I asked groups to brainstorm at least 10 different ideas for Field Notes. To begin the process I shared some less obvious examples of potential Note topics, along with the information that all notes would have a text component in addition to images or other multimedia created by students.

> I might consider making a Sound Note of different sounds I hear or overhear while waiting for the trolley. Or maybe a Nature Note about unseen wildness in the city. Or a Food Note about a food and memory that have special meaning to me. Or maybe a Culture or Relationship Note. Remember they are looking for new narratives and understandings, new ways of looking at the city and different issues you face. In table groups, take 5 minutes to create your own lists.

As groups talked and wrote, I was active, popping up at different tables when conversation seemed to wane, scanning over what they had on their papers, and deciding if they would benefit from me asking brief questions to help them move forward. "The idea of a Culture Note sounds great. Can you make that more specific? Tell me more what you were thinking."

The quality of individual table brainstorm lists was mixed and I found some of the entries confusing. I tried to remedy this by sitting at the computer next to the projector and having students share highlights out loud. As individuals spoke up I recorded their ideas on a doc that they could see on the projector and would later be able to view on their own. Some ideas I added directly to the list. For others, I asked for clarification and explanation before I wrote, sometimes renaming the note along with the student before typing. I used this stage as an opportunity to bring students back to the goals of the project.

> "Bus stop note is an interesting one, Samerah. Before I write it, can you explain how that fits into the idea of multiple histories or new narratives or understandings?"
>
> I walk a fine line here, wanting to encourage but also trying to guide Samerah and all the students toward more complex ideas.
>
> "Sure. This is the stop I've waited at all my life. The neighborhood around it has changed a lot but the guy who runs the corner store behind the stop has been there forever and I've known him since I started kindergarten."

"I love it. So this is a Bus Stop Note but also might be a Neighborhood Note or maybe even a Relationship Note?"

"You could say that." Samerah is understandably a little resistant to my attempt to change the title of her Note but my goal is to make sure that she and all the students are beginning to see the Notes as opportunities to take everyday, seemingly simple aspects of their lives and document them in a way that reveals complexity and nuance.

By the end of our brainstorming process, students had access to an impressive array of possibilities for their own work. Some of the more unexpected ideas included Street Notes of alleyways, Hair Notes, Religion Notes, and Individuality Notes. Some of the ideas were quirky. Others spoke to what felt like crucial issues in students' lives. I was beginning to feel more confident about the project but knew that each of the following steps would have to be strategic in order to lead to success. I was hoping for work that would be both creative and intellectual, allowing students to affirm themselves and their realities.

The class had moved past initial doubts about a new project into a phase of collective, albeit still somewhat subdued, excitement about what they could create. An important aspect of this phase is that it had reshaped the normal hierarchy of school success. Many students who did not typically display enthusiasm about their academic work had ideas that they were eager to pursue. The entry bar had shifted, and a student who did not have confidence in his writing was excited about his Note on skateboard culture. Another student who had missed several recent assignments was already talking to friends about interviewing them for a Hijabi Note.

Some of the initial excitement was about the multimedia that students were planning to make to accompany their Notes. These short films, photos, or audio were an integral part of the project but I sensed danger that the multimedia might replace the writing that was meant to be an essential component of the work. I designed checkpoints with this in mind. The initial step was for students to write a proposal for their first Note. I gave students a template for proposals, asking them to articulate their goals for the Note and how it would connect to the goals of the project, and to explain the process for making the note and the steps for its completion. I traveled through the room during days that students worked on proposals, but I wanted this stage to be initiated by them so I only sat down with students who seemed to be struggling to help them identify early ideas. I knew I would have the chance to help students expand or refine their ideas in conferences about their completed proposals.

Frequently, I tried to leverage the fact that this individual work was part of a larger, communal project. At the beginning of each class, I asked two students developing unique note ideas to share their ideas out loud with everyone. One day, strategically, when students seemed to be losing focus as they worked on proposals, I asked students to pause and asked Siani to share what I knew was her insightful thinking behind her Hijabi Note. (She was intent on showing that her Muslim friends wore Hijabs to feel comfortable with themselves, even though it makes them stand out in wider U.S. society.) Pauses like this allow students to be inspired by the work of their peers, get people excited about the collective aspect of the project, and serve to focus students while helping those who have not yet added depth to their own ideas.

Students had to conference with me in order to get credit and approval to proceed. These conferences provided me with an opportunity to kindly challenge each student to improve the quality of the note they were planning to write. As students sat with me, I heard similar questions coming out of my mouth:

Can you explain that more? What do you mean?
How does that connect to the project goals?
Why is this important? What are you trying to communicate to
   readers?
Is another way of saying that _____ ?

The dynamics of each conference depended on the personality of the student. Some students embraced the opportunity to receive feedback and think about ways to revise their ideas, while with others I realized the need to step back a bit and asked a minimal number of questions, hoping to not overwhelm them but rather provide a morsel that might influence the final product in a positive way. As I sat down next to Rob, he immediately started talking about the skateboard documentary he had already started making. "This is how people gather in the city and people that don't skate don't know anything about it!" This was the most invested Rob has been in his work all year. I listened to his ideas for a bit as I strategized about ways to encourage him and help him make his Note more complex. After affirming his idea, I told him I had a couple of questions and asked him to write them in his doc to help guide the written component of his note. I made a point of reminding him that he gets to choose how to frame it but that I did think he needed to go further than merely showing people skateboarding. "What different things draw people to skating? What does it mean to be part of a subculture? Is there something about belonging that is important here? Does skating tell us something about different people's views of the city?" I tried to give him a range of starting points or threads that I hoped he would carry forward. He expressed mild interest in some of what I said but, feeling pressure to move on to my next conference, I was not sure about the status of the Note he was developing. I recognize now that it may not have been possible to steer his enthusiasm for his film to also include deeper analysis or reflection. There is a benefit to letting students pursue work they are passionate about, even if the project structure does not fully correspond to teacher expectations. Rob lost some points in his final project grade for not including very much analysis (he did include some) but he produced his most polished piece of work of the year, building his confidence and expanding his sense of self. He proudly shared his video with many outside of our classroom.

In the culminating days of the project, most students had given in to the joy of creating work that mattered to them. There were claps and cheers each time I displayed a new Field Note that had been published on the site by the project coordinators. I had students come to the front of the room at the beginning of classes, reading excerpts from their Notes, sharing videos they made, photos they took, and audio they recorded. The successes were collective as people called out supportively each time a student shared. In a way that seemed almost magical, the sum of their work did seem to represent new narratives and understandings.

During this last week of the project the rest of class time was devoted to students completing their final Notes; they edited each other's work to get it to the point where I agreed it could be sent out, they edited video, and they rushed to complete details necessary to have their work included as part of the larger collaborative project which, in a beautiful way, seemed to have taken on a life of its own. (The project website can be seen at tinyurl.com/tfald8.) I was asked to write an intro to the work and choose excerpts from student Field Notes for Primary Sources, the exhibition handbook:

Teenagers have unique perspectives on our city. They exist in a liminal zone, not yet expected to inhabit the adult world, yet beyond childhood. They move around independently, eager to observe and question. My Science Leadership Academy students bring a wide range of Philly experiences and perspectives to the

Re-PLACE-ing project.

Katia came to Philly in 2012 from Algeria not knowing any English. She had to learn to exist in a new culture and a new language while negotiating a vision impairment. Her Vision Note reminds us that blindness is not a limitation. She describes how she learned to navigate a new city and all that she knows, feels, and experiences when out on the street.

"Blindness is Not a Limitation" by Katia

It is true that my eyes do not see as well as yours, but humans have other senses that you may take for granted. Don't worry, I know when to go and when to stop. You look around in all directions, but I do not even have to turn my head; the sound of the engine reveals the speed, distance, and direction. When I make a move I know for sure that it's safe.

Ava used to play in the rubble of Northern Liberties. Her Street Note asks readers to see the "ghosts of her past," now buried under a condo complex which speaks, "I used to be something else." What was once a sanctuary has become memory.

"Northern Liberties" by Ava

The location of those condos used to be the go-to place for all the neighborhood kids to play and dream new adventures, but all people see now are giant, modern buildings. I want everyone to know that we used to play there and that the ghosts of our past remain there playing indefinitely while new tenants live their everyday lives.

Jade is drawn to the contrast of a sunrise and a piece of trash in the street. She imagines a story behind this worthless object and contemplates "the pieces of ourselves we lose in all the motions of our daily lives." She suggests that our problem with litter may also be a problem of forgotten memories.

"The Things We Ignore" by Jade

As city folks we are always rushing through our activities and sometimes we lose pieces of ourselves in all the motions of our daily lives. These pieces are piling up in gutters all over the city, taking on a life of their own. The more frightening part of all this is not that things are forgotten or discarded, but that we don't seem to notice. The clutter seems so unimportant. We walk through a city of trash and forgotten memories without a second glance.

Looking at this work as a collection, the Notes students created provided opportunities for young people to reexamine and fully claim their lived realities. These examinations were frequently avenues for affirmation of students' experiences as student authors reflected deeply on their lives and developed products to express their understandings. At other times students used the Notes to challenge readers to understand and make space for their identities, understandings, and ways of living.

OUR PHILADELPHIA, OUR AMERICA

Partway into a different school year, following the presidential election of 2016, I was struggling. There were regular reports about increases in the number of hate crimes throughout the United States. People in my community and across the country were trying to figure out how to respond to what seemed to be changing rules of social discourse. No longer could we look to the top levels of government and expect a facade of civility and condemnation of certain forms of extremism. I felt depleted by this state of affairs, but could not tell how my students were being impacted. Whether they were tuned in to national political news or not, I wanted them to be able to create work that spoke to their experiences at that historical moment. I looked to design a project that could be an avenue for affirming and expanding students' own knowledge and experiences rather than merely creating something to meet outside criteria.

In my classes, things seemed to be going well on some levels. Our classroom community felt cohesive. Throughout the semester we had read two novels, deeply investigating the experiences of immigrants and refugees. The students had completed papers and projects, taught lessons, and had numerous smaller assignments and discussions. This all did not feel like enough to address the current moment. Some journal entries and discussions had focused on recent changes in our country, but students had not completed work that pushed them to explore their own narratives or understandings at a time that felt to me as if our country was being steered toward a cliff.

I began to plan for the next part of the semester. I also reached out to Amal Giknis, a colleague who was teaching the other half of the 12th grade at my school. She shared my desire to have students produce work that allowed them to reflect on their realities and speak to the current moment. Our visions did not align perfectly, but we realized this did not matter. We could start a grade-wide project even as the approach in our classes would be slightly different. Using the Re-PLACE-ing project as a model, we came up with the idea for the "Our Philadelphia, Our America" project. We would use the model of written Field Notes and create a site where students were able to post their own work. We would not have the benefit of an outside organization to sponsor the project or other artists to participate, but students would know that they work they published would be seen by others in their grade and visible to a larger audience on the web.

Before classes began, we problem-solved to avoid pitfalls that could sabotage the project. We needed to set up a workflow and to institute some form of quality control so that work was not posted until it had been revised and met certain standards. This project was exciting in its breadth and the amount of choice that it would provide, but we knew that not all students would instantly have ideas that they would want to write about. Some students would want to be creative, others to be political, and still others would not know what they wanted to do. We needed model texts that would help us frame the project, and we would require the initial stages of the work to be communal, allowing us all to brainstorm and borrow ideas from each other.

Amal's students were reading *Citizen* by Claudia Rankine (2015), which she was planning to use as a model text. My class had just finished the book *Exit West* by Mohsin Hamid (2017), but I needed additional texts to help provoke ideas and to provide models of different types of writing. I settled on excerpts from *Leaves of Grass* by Walt Whitman (2005) and *Hope in the Dark* by Rebecca Solnit (2016). Each text was provocative in its own way, and would help students think about new forms of expression and different ways of being in the world. I was hoping the texts and discussions would push students to think about the relationships between individuals and the wider world, sparking ideas for their own writing.

Amal and I worked together to write a description of the project that would match both of our visions and our desire to have students speak to the current moment:

Our Philadelphia, Our America Project Description

As young people in Philadelphia you bring unique perspectives to the current and future state of our communities, our city, and our country. For this project, you will be creating a series of Field Notes that speak to current issues, your notions of necessary understandings, and your lived reality. You can think of these Field Notes as a way to make public who we are, what we think we believe, and what we know. Each Field Note will include a creative/descriptive and an analytical component.

Guiding Questions for the Project

- How can we respond to this moment in time?
- What new narratives can we construct in order to re-imagine future possibilities?
- What does it mean to be a citizen?
- What does it mean to be a young person in Philadelphia?

Ideas to Emphasize

- Contrasts & Contradictions
- Different Realities
- Hidden & Unseen
- Untold Stories

Field Notes

For the sake of this project, Field Notes consist of a combination of text (at least 500 words) and multimedia (video, audio, photos, or artwork created by you). During this last part of the semester you will be creating three Field Notes that will be posted to the Our Philadelphia, Our America site. One important note: two of the Field Notes can be about your own experiences and one must be about someone else's experiences or something unfamiliar to you. All 12th-graders will be participating in this project, and the final product will be shared with a public audience.

Workflow for Each Field Note:

- Complete proposal form
- Conference with teacher and get approval

- Write draft
- Complete Self-Eval & Peer Review Form (see Appendix section C)
- Revise
- Conference with teacher for final feedback
- Revise
- Create multimedia
- Post to site as draft
- Check formatting and professionalism
- Post

As with the Re-PLACE-ing project, the process began by having students brainstorm ideas and the creation of a communal list that was meant to provide a wide range of ideas and inspiration. The sequence of steps we asked students to follow was designed to push students to submit the highest-quality work possible. Students would be creating their work in community with others, sharing their own drafts and reading the rough work of others. These steps also established multiple opportunities for me to check in with students about their work, assisting those who were struggling and providing feedback to those who had a steady workflow. Students were expected to complete three Field Notes throughout the course of the project. For students who had a hard time with writing activities, I told them on the side that I could grade them for two high-quality Field Notes rather than have them rushing to attempt to do three.

Once students began to post Notes, they also began to appreciate the work of their peers as I put the final products on the projector and had authors share their work aloud. This allowed the project to gather its own momentum, helping those who were struggling to develop ideas and inspiration. Posting notes required some attention to certain tech details. In each class I appointed three "tech czars." These students were the point people that others turned to for help publishing their work to the project website once they worked through all the steps of creating a Field Note and received permission to post.

The scope of the work was impressive when put together; the hundreds of Field Notes ranged from intimate to comic, inspiring to quirky. The parent who was in charge of the Twitter account for our Home and School Association eagerly tweeted out descriptions and links to different Field Notes over the course of a couple weeks, often resulting in giddy students who would report their posts had received multiple comments.

Below are some excerpts from Our Philadelphia, Our America. (Full project can be seen at: tinyurl.com/tfald9).

CJ's **Assimilation Note** reflects on the contrasts and different pressures of assimilation in her life as a Sierra Leonean immigrant:

> A symphony of drums pulsated underneath my bare feet as I circled the wooden floor. Yvonne Chaka Chaka's classic "Umqombothi" blasted through our radio. I could hear my grandparents' hearty laughs echoing off the walls as I shuffled across the room, every so often tightening the lappa around my waist. My grandmother then took my hand to dance and we hit the fiercest Azonto, to the tune of my uncle's rickety guitar in the background. She wore her gravity-defying headpiece like a crown and woven bangles cascaded down her arms. In the morning, we would wake up to the stifling reality of poverty and conflict, but in that moment, all we knew was rhythm. All I knew was life and prevailing peace.
>
> Born to a Fulani mother and Mandingo father, my joy was inherited. Born during a civil war, my joy became a survival instinct. Fingers locked, my grandmother guided me around the dining room for another hour, belting "Obulamu Bwakisela" or "Life is too short." Just waking up was a reason to celebrate in Freetown, Sierra Leone.
>
> Over 4,000 miles from my hometown, I find myself still at times forgetting that I am in another country. Sub-Saharan African Flags line up several blocks throughout Woodland, Philadelphia, known as "Little Africa." Large baskets overflowing with ornate textiles can usually be found outside little shops at every turn. The shelves of my uncle's market are stacked with products from Sierra Leone, Nigeria, the Ivory Coast, and other neighboring countries . . . My family is poor but most joyful and we still don't need a reason to celebrate life. The fact that our values have not dispersed in an effort to assimilate is a testament to the endurance of my culture.

Fatima's **Street Note** describes the experience of being a young woman who is regularly catcalled by men on the street:

> "Hey pretty what's your name?"
>
> As I turn the corner there is a group of boys standing right in front of the Papi store. I couldn't believe this was happening, it was only 8 am. I had my Nike slippers on with my hair tied up. When I get closer to the door he gets closer to me trying to touch my face . . .
>
> "Where you going? I'm talking to you."
>
> "Why you walking so fast?"
>
> He looks at me with a grin while I yank my arm from him.

"I don't want you. Can you leave me alone?"

"So you can't talk? Oh for real, okay? I ain't want you anyway."

"You just came at me like three seconds ago."

I never understood why guys get upset when a woman rejects them. Language is a special thing . . . Catcalling is another language that people use to try to get a girl who can fulfill their desires. Catcalling is a serious thing because you are disrespecting a woman by shouting or making a sexual comment towards her. Catcalling is a form of harassment. Some men believe women ask for it, but nobody asks for a man to disrespect her in public . . .

Guys don't want to know our names. They always use the lines "What's your name?" or, "Sweetheart, tell me your name." When you refuse to give them your name they call you disrespectful names based on their hurt and rejection.

You're mad because I didn't give you my name? If you knew my name what would have been different? Would a commitment be formed? These are the things that women think about . . .

Taya's **Work Note** is about the overwhelming reality of balancing her many hours working in a job with her student responsibilities and integrates excerpts from Walt Whitman (*in italics*):

4:00 AM

My alarm goes off like sirens ringing in my ears. I reach quickly to turn it off. My eyes can barely open as I take deep and heavy breaths while forcing my body to stand up. Thirty minutes into my dreadful morning I caught a quick burst of life! *"The feeling of health, the full-noon trill, the song of me rising from bed and meeting the sun."* It excites me as the wind smoothly caress my face and gives me a feeling of being alive!

7:00 AM

Running down the street, trying my very best not to miss another bus. I can't be late to school. Three previous latenesses overtake my mind and force me to get to school on time; no breakfast stops or time to waste.

8:15 AM

First period, American Government, is filled with long articles and primary sources. Lectures and assignments seem to flood the next five periods. By second period the symptoms begin to hit. Every article becomes blurred in my head and words begin to switch order.

As each period goes by it is now time for advisory. A time I use to relax and occasionally catch up on all the blurred words that my eyes may have missed earlier. I feel a sense of relief, a time where I feel I have no troubles. *"What is that you express in your eyes? It seems to me more than all the print I have read in my life."* The more I relax the more my life seems to unravel.

3:50 PM

Relaxation quickly dissolves and it's time to get to work. I have approximately an hour to get from school to my job. Trolley to the Market-Frankford Line to the 58 bus. All to arrive at a place I have no interest in being at.

5:00 PM

I clock in and begin my lonely work. Folding shirts becomes repetitive as the colors all seem to blend. My head goes down into my shirt before I can realize this is not the place or time to fall asleep. I walk around trying to regain my visual comprehension of my surroundings . . .

11:00 PM

Time to clock out! A time that seemed so far is right in front of me. I call an uber, waiting anxiously for it to arrive so I can feel the warmth of my house. I anticipate the smell of food as I walk through the door. It pulls up . . .

This is a life of a working student, no breaks, no time to be tired, just a continuous ongoing day. Every day is worse than the last and you seem more and more dead as the weeks go by. Until your body drops and you feel like you have no control over anything that happens. You can't feel anything but the burning of your eyes as they close and tingles of your fingertips as your hand lays face down on your bed. It is never over.

This type of project can be understood as an exercise in decolonization. The students wrote about crucial and sometimes disturbing issues in their lives, centering their ideas, experiences, and voices. While the project had clear criteria, their thoughts were not mediated. Instead, divergent thinking was encouraged and students found ways to question powerful systems. Their creations represented their values, their preoccupations, and the complexity of their lives.

CODA

Schools reflect societies. When school design and pathways for learning are not designed with the intention of creating opportunities for discovery, the results are oppressive. This chapter begins with a quote from Audre Lorde (1998): "What are the words you do not yet have? What do you need to say?" She then reveals a universal truth: "[T]he transformation of silence into language and action is an act of self-revelation" (p. 41). When learning is designed in ways that push students toward creative, insightful language and action, we bear witness to something truly revelatory. These experiences result in learning that reclaims and sustains rather than demanding conformity. Students view the dominant culture and their places in the world differently, challenging dominant or unexplored narratives, figuring out along the way what it is that they want to say and then receiving the reactions and affirmations of others for sharing their words in public ways. This is what happens when we change our understandings of what it means to construct knowledge, working to decolonize classroom learning while creating the conditions for students to succeed as themselves. This is what it means to practice a humanizing pedagogy that affirms the complexity of our world and students' lives.

CHAPTER 6

The Multiple Realities of Teaching for a Living Democracy

> When you recognize uncertainty, you recognize that you may be able to influence the outcomes.
>
> —Rebecca Solnit, 2016

The types of teaching described in this book change what it means to work with students. The complicated nature of this work means that it is rare that I feel fully at ease or entirely successful at the end of a day of teaching. Even on days when things went well, some of my time with students involved uncertainty or struggle. As much as I want the work to be a shared endeavor, it is impossible to ignore the fact that school is part of a compulsory system. In the eyes of students, I am a gatekeeper, supporting or hindering their desire for success and their future aspirations. In the midst of this dynamic exist multiple layers of intellectual exploration and project-based learning that immerse us in the complicated, often messy realities of authentic work.

Teaching is unique in both potential and challenges. Carla Shalaby describes aspects of this in *Troublemakers*: "In no other profession do people have the opportunity to literally create a parallel world—a world that is safer, fairer, freer" (2017, p. 80). In an earlier time period, activist and abolitionist Frederick Douglass (1857) delineated the necessity of friction within the process of change: "If there is no struggle there is no progress" (1857). Possibility and struggle are ingredients for growth, but engaging with both means learners will feel discomfort, creating challenges for students and teachers.

This chapter explores both the vision of creative possibility I have been depicting and the inevitable friction that results when transgressive learning experiences engage layers of student identity and social issues. Another way to think of this is as an examination of the unfinished edges that are so much a part of a teaching practice based on connection and real-world work. The examples are meant to illustrate some of the different responses and strategies available to teachers in these difficult moments, to use frustration and struggle to inform and inspire new approaches rather than to become entrenched in the traditional power dynamics that can divide students and teachers.

LEARNING IN ACTION: ART IN THE OPEN

Several years ago, I began a partnership with the Leah Stein Dance Company. Together, we designed a project where students would immerse themselves in the process of creating and performing site-specific dance pieces. This project challenged students to engage creatively and pushed them outside their comfort zones. During the project it was unclear if the undertaking would succeed and the public performances would be successful. Now I offer it as an example of an art-based project where finding ways to navigate the inherent messiness of creativity allowed students to produce compelling finished products.

With the goals of having students investigate the questions *Why do people create art?* and *What makes art powerful?* we planned to have student groups choreograph their own performance pieces. These pieces would use the techniques taught to them by the professional dancers to create movements and sounds inspired by various outdoor locations. Ultimately, we hoped that the dances would be performed for audiences as part of a city-wide arts festival.

After an initial workshop where the dancers introduced students to the skills and techniques required for the work, student groups spent class time at outdoor sites of their choosing. When the dancers and I visited the sites in the early stages of creation, we regularly found groups of young people doubting themselves, the process, and the project. They questioned whether they needed to write about and deeply observe their site as they learned to do in the workshop. They were hesitant to inhabit their bodies in physical and playful ways, a necessity for the project. Once we found a student group seated in various parts of their site in a residential alleyway. One girl was intently focused on her phone, and two others were having a private conversation together, while the other group members were staring off into space.

This was the messy stage! Groups were not accomplishing very much, individuals were not communicating effectively, and there was little engagement or commitment to the project. In a similar fashion to what I do with groups during classroom-based projects, the dancers and I provided support by bringing the groups together, asking questions, and selectively modeling. During these conferences the students saw the dancers creating movements and sounds in their site, often building on the small movement gestures or elements the students had created on their own. Before we left each site we were sure to assign specific tasks to students to help them progress in this early stage of the process of creation.

Days later, after multiple consultations, regular encouragement, and the sharing of ideas among groups, performance day neared. Groups had taken ownership of the process. The same 10th-graders who had been staring at their phones or off into space physically engaged with their site and each other, repeatedly rehearsing, modifying, and adding to the dance they were creating. They worked to coordinate the sequencing and timing of their piece, repeating a move where the four of them leaned together before pushing off and spreading out to positions against trees, hydrants, and fences at different locations in their alley. Each time they rehearsed, they shared ideas for revisions, offering regular feedback with the goal of creating a more polished performance.

By performance day, the students' mood of reluctant, moderate participation of 2 weeks earlier has been replaced. Groups arrive with costumes, their dance pieces have titles, and every group is preparing for the two time slots in which they are scheduled to perform. There is very little for the teacher-artists to do beyond wishing everyone luck and congratulating them on all they accomplished.

At the designated hour other students (the audience) excitedly flow out of the school to join audience members from the arts festival. Everyone holds the maps and schedules for the performances for our school's contribution to the city-wide Art in the Open Festival. One group of student dancers is dressed in black T-shirts and black pants. They are positioned against orange metal benches on a platform over the Schuylkill River. Another group is hidden behind trees that line the pathways of a small public garden that many members of the school community never noticed despite its close proximity to our building.

The performances combine unique movements and sounds, all generated within the sites. At the culmination of one performance a student stands still in front of the other members of his group, powerfully upright under a grimy overpass, a symbol of power with his face turned upward, arms fully extended, fingers stretching. In the middle of a different performance, the group in a public garden forms a close circle, arms around each other's shoulders, swaying together while creating rhythmic sounds. The range of movements, sounds, sites, and creativity is quirky and exciting. Performers have found ways to carry themselves with confidence, often fluidly coordinated with other members of their group. Audiences at each performance are drawn into the dances, responding with enthusiastic cheers. (A video documenting the process can be seen at tinyurl.com/tfald10.)

THE MESSY PROCESS OF CREATION

The dance project felt risky. Students were asked to immerse themselves in a creative process that was new and uncomfortable. They were doing challenging and stimulating work that was beyond my own expertise, work that depended on the counsel of outside experts. The structure combined with the independence provided allowed them to improve their skills of observation, collaborate deeply with others, and have an authentic experience of creating unique art. All of these elements were reinforced and deepened by writing students produced during and after the project. Importantly, the public aspects of the project made the work gain a level of authenticity and added to feelings of pride and success at the end.

The changes over different stages of this project show what regularly happens when young people are asked to create. Early in the process, there is often a lack of direction or focus. If there is a cohesive and engaging structure, the process evolves, the work advances, and focus and collaboration increase. Scaffolding and support or a safety net are needed along with the opportunity for individuals or groups to experience and move through feelings of being stuck or overwhelmed.

In my classroom, there are also frequently days when my check-ins with students reveal that young people are lost or unsure how to proceed with the early stages of a project:

"What topic are you going to focus on?" I ask Keith as I kneel down next him.

"I can't decide. I'm stuck," he mumbles, leaning forward and staring straight into his computer screen as he talks.

I resist my desire to chastise him for not utilizing the list of topic ideas we generated as a class. Other students have it on the table in front of them but his notebook seems to have disappeared. I also don't see any of the rough writing that I assumed he had been doing along with his classmates over the previous 2 days. Knowing that there are other students waiting to speak with me, I force myself to sit longer with Keith and try to help him identify a way to move forward with the work.

"Well, to start, which of the topics that we were discussing seemed interesting to you?" I know that if I immediately begin to suggest topics he will likely remain stuck but if I can help him identify something of his own choosing and we can agree on a step-by-step plan to move forward, he is much more likely to get himself out of this hole.

There are other times when I look around the room and see that it is not just one or two but many students who don't have a clear vision of their process or the final product they are working toward. The room is filled with exasperation and frustration. At the end of these class periods, I find myself doubting both my planning and project design. I try to maintain an understanding of process and decipher what is happening. I remind myself that friction is not inherently bad—meaningful work often produces cognitive discomfort, an organic part of learning and creating.

I structure class periods to avoid unproductive struggles if possible. At the beginnings of units we work together as a whole group, reading, investigating, and discussing. My goals are to establish a collective background understanding of a topic and to identify different paths of inquiry. Later come the early design and drafting days of projects. These class periods are filled with random ideas, questions, changing minds, and students who feel unsure. I make sure that I am actively engaging with different students in order to provide regular assistance. The final stages of projects are when students and groups focus on specific, clearly defined tasks, which are required to bring their project-based work to fruition. These days there is often a checklist on the board or students have made a to-do list of their own. Everyone has clearly defined tasks to complete.

At times when the frustration feels like it is less a result of the inherent trajectory of authentic inquiry and creation and more about personal or interpersonal issues, I will reach out to specific students or sit down at the table with a group that seems to be struggling. Although I will not be able to fully eliminate the messy stages of creation, I can learn more, developing a fuller understanding of the dynamics at work and different ways I can respond, thereby better helping students progress with their work. According to Rifah, a former student who shared her thoughts about classroom dynamics with me, "The first step should be understanding the difference between what the students actually need versus what you (the teacher) think that they need. The easiest way to spot the difference is to just talk to your students!"

It always helps to recall the frustration I feel at times when I am in the midst of a project of my own. In these moments I muck around, turn to others, and search out examples as I slowly figure out my own path. Recognizing this helps me fully understand and embrace the inherent struggles that students need to experience in order to create complex work. If I do not allow learning to be risky and messy, I eliminate authentic experiences for students as thinkers and creators. The dance project felt overwhelming throughout much of the process and required intensive check-ins and serious nudging in order to move students past their early resistance and hesitation. Despite my recollections of struggle, years later when I see those students this is always the first project they excitedly recall.

NAVIGATING INTOLERANCE

During a unit investigating the idea of "crossing boundaries" I came into class excited and proud of what I felt was a bold choice. Students were in the early stages of creating podcasts in which they would interview someone outside of the school community about their personal experiences of crossing boundaries. The class had discussed the nature of different racial boundaries in the novel *Passing* by Nella Larsen (1997, originally published 1929), which we had just completed; we had brainstormed a range of boundaries that people chose to, or are forced to, cross in their lives; and each student had proposed the subject whom they intended to interview for their project.

This was the day we would begin examining the genre of podcasts and discuss some of the technical aspects of creating audio work. I had chosen an example to share with the class that would expose them to high-quality technical work but also expose them to a reality many of them knew little about: trans and nonbinary gender identities. I was proud of my choice and undoubtedly feeling overconfident about my power to impact my students.

Shortly after I began playing the radio story about a transgender child and a family's journey to understand a gender identity that defied traditional norms, things started to go wrong. I paused the audio frequently to ask students what they were noticing, but every time I hit play Brittany would begin muttering comments in response to what she was hearing. "This is crazy." "No way." The comments sent a clear message of intolerance and disapproval about the story she was hearing about someone whose identity does not conform to the construct of a gender binary.

I tried to manage the situation and felt forced into damage control mode. "Brittany, please don't talk while we're all listening." She kept muttering and I gave her my harshest look: "That's enough."

Her comments continued and my anger grew. It was becoming clear that she either was not going to, or somehow could not, stop her negativity and disapproval. At this point the class's attention and my own had shifted from the podcast's content to the battle between myself and Brittany. Stepping fully into my authority as teacher, unable to restrain my anger any longer, I raised my voice. "If you can't be respectful, you need to leave the room. Now! We'll all wait for you." It was a dreaded moment of confrontation playing out in front of an entire class. Luckily for me she wanted out of this situation as much as I wanted her out. "Fuck this shit. I'm out," she spoke under her breath as she grabbed her belongings and stormed out the door.

My heart was pounding and my frustration was undoubtedly obvious to the rest of the class. I had planned a class with the intent of exposing students to what is for many a misunderstood reality. My intent had been that students would gain an understanding of the technical requirements of a podcast along with some insight into the ways social norms of gender identity often oppress people, but instead the lesson had turned into a power struggle between me and a student. I continued class in the most normal voice I could muster.

When I was able to sit down in my empty classroom and regroup once students had left, my phone rang. It was Brittany's mom. The parents wanted to meet to discuss what had happened. I felt defeated by the fact that the lesson had been derailed and intolerance had been openly expressed and now also felt dread about how this meeting would play out. I talked to other teachers who knew Brittany to learn more about her and her family, hoping to gain insights about how to best approach the meeting and work with this family rather than be pitted against them.

The next day Brittany's parents arrived determined to defend their daughter's behavior. We sat at a table in my classroom, Brittany seated to the left of her father, staring down at the floor. Her mother looked directly at me and spoke strongly as her husband nodded along. "Brittany has never been kicked out of a class in all of her years of school. We raised her well and she knows how to behave. We can't understand why this happened in your class."

It was clear that this was a moment that would largely determine the trajectory of the rest of my year with Brittany. I still felt the residue of my anger and disappointment about the ways she had sabotaged the lesson the previous day. In the morning, having processed the experience, I tried to reconnect with her but she had responded to my "Good morning" by staring ahead silently as she entered my classroom.

"Yesterday was a hard day for us," I began, "but I want to acknowledge that Brittany is a very talented young woman who has had many wonderful moments in class this year." There was still tension in the room but establishing this container of care and appreciation led to a palpable shift. Despite large differences, we were able to begin to approach this conflict not as enemies but as people with a shared investment in and appreciation for Brittany.

I explained the entire scenario of the previous day's class to her parents. "Our family doesn't share the views of that radio piece, but we also don't support disrespectful behavior from Brittany," replied her dad. "Brittany, you are going to need to apologize. And then tell us, the next time you feel uncomfortable with something in class, how are you going to deal with it?"

During the meeting I managed to contain my own hurt in a way that allowed the conflict to transform into an opportunity for validation of a young woman and a parent-prompted, student-generated plan for the future. The family had not demanded tolerance from Brittany, but they had made it clear that she needed to respect the learning environment. They stopped short of challenging my curriculum choices despite their disapproval of the content.

I reflected on the choices I made. Sharing the podcast was not an attempt to shock or offend but to educate and provide a window into lesser-known realities. While I wish the conflict with Brittany hadn't occurred in front of the rest of the class, the conflict did seem to be an inevitable aspect of work that challenges oppressive social norms. I didn't want to alienate a student but there needed to be a way for us to use class to investigate what were, for some, issues that challenged beliefs from home or religious institutions. If I labeled any student solely based on an intolerant view or an undesirable behavior, I would lose the opportunity to work with them in meaningful ways. Internally I confirmed the need to continue my search for ways to affirm the humanity of students, while also challenging them to engage with new ideas and understandings as part of our processes of inquiry.

ENGAGING ISSUES OF THE WORLD

This final example of classroom potential and challenge took place during a very difficult time. The previous night the grand jury in Ferguson, MO, had announced that there would be no indictment against officer Darren Wilson in the shooting death of Michael Brown. Social media was ablaze with rage and despair. The morning was gray and the energy in the room reflected the fact that Thanksgiving break was 2 days away.

Usually I plan so that class discussions are preceded by writing, reading, or small-group discussion, giving students a chance to develop their thoughts. This day felt different. There was something raw in the air. I needed to address it and provide a structure that would allow us to process as a group. As George Lakey says, "When a conflict erupts near you, move closer" (2013). This moment felt like it demanded an opportunity for students to express emotions and beliefs about race, violence, despair, and U.S. society.

I perched atop a stool in the front of the room and referenced the news from the night before, asking, "What different things have you all heard?" Some students sat slumped in their seats while others looked around with curiosity. None of us knew what would happen or where the conversation would lead. My strategy was to frame the conversation around knowledge of the events and acknowledgment of injustice. Rather than hearing extensively from me, students needed space to voice what they knew and felt while hearing their classmates' perspectives. This was a time to develop consciousness related to the events and emotion of the day.

The discussion began slowly with information from different people and questions about the sequence of events. I let students respond to each other whenever possible, sometimes offering a comment with additional information when it seemed clear that there were gaps in knowledge about how events had unfolded. After everyone was caught up on what had transpired, I asked for additional observations about the protests and commentary students had heard in different places: "What have you noticed about this event or about what is being said online and in your communities?" I intentionally asked the question this way, wanting students to feel an openness to sharing ideas but trying to steer students away from what in that moment would feel like fruitless interpersonal debates.

After some students tested the water, it became clear to others that a container existed for them to share and that previously established classroom norms of active listening meant ideas would be taken in by the group. This feeling was due, in part, to the ways that people who spoke were being affirmed by me and others. Students were quick to tune in to each other because they sensed the importance and gravity of the events. The fact that the discussion began with a clear intent of creating space for students to express themselves signified an opening.

"What's going to make it stop? We need to be treated like people!" exclaimed Simone, a biracial girl, as she responded to a boy who felt that the situation was over and done. She wasn't crying but we could all sense the depth of emotion and the tears close to the surface. As the discussion continued, I facilitated, doing my best to fully acknowledge what people were saying while paying attention to the flow of the conversation, the experience of participants, and what my colleague Matthew Kay calls the "loose threads" (2018). At times I offered the group a strategic question to deepen the discussion, but I was wary of taking up too much space, knowing that it was important for many students to be able to express themselves. I was aware that most of the students in the room shared feelings of justified indignation and despair. I was also aware that in the room there were children (of different races) who had parents who were police officers and prison guards. They undoubtedly had different layers of emotions and responses. I knew I had to facilitate the conversation without forgetting that I bring my own social status and perceptions to this moment in U.S. history. There is not one simple or common language that we all share, and it would be inappropriate to expect some version of a flawless class or an idyllic outcome.

The space I inhabit at any moment is not neutral. Rather, I am aware of a complex and conflicting array of student needs that I strive to recognize and respect. In a moment when official structures in our society condone the pointless death of an African American youth, no one should be denied their grief or rage and there is a strong need to validate it. I looked for openings to acknowledge sorrow and fear that people felt, but maintained awareness of my goal of pushing students toward complex and critically nuanced views of society, sometimes asking people to explain ideas more fully or to avoid generalizations. Another consideration as I attempted to create space and, when necessary, steer the discussion, is that it would have been foolish for me to ignore the fact that many of my students of color were impacted more intimately than others in the room by this event. They are required to live their lives with the knowledge that their identities mean facing risk in our society. This moment reminded many that there is rarely accountability for racist acts by government agents. This is information some of my white students had been able to ignore, but needed to be able to hear and understand. For this reason, I paid particular attention to affirming voices and ideas that are too often marginalized.

The discussion often felt rough, alternating between poignant moments, affirmations, and times when I felt a lack of larger direction or cohesiveness. While I tried to make space for a mixture of voices and maintain a container, I know that some students stayed silent because they were reluctant or afraid to contribute to a difficult discussion in a mixed group at an overwhelming time.

While it is important to acknowledge the ways a discussion or lesson falls short, it is also clear that commitment to creating space allows students to use classroom discussions and experiences as tools for their own affirmation and transformation. This is the result of intentional use of strategy and design combined with the humility necessary to guide a group toward honest sharing of themselves, their despair, and their questions about the society they are growing up in. In the same way that young people's lives can be altered by new knowledge of self and the development of feelings of agency, teaching that does not acknowledge students' realities and society's failings can quickly replicate oppressive structures.

CODA

The reality of working with young people in our complex, unequal society means that days will be filled with joy, creativity, struggle, and conflict. I hope that the examples in this chapter capture some different approaches for navigating these uncertainties. It is through challenging moments that students discover new understandings of themselves and their world.

Ultimately these moments are what it means to teach in a democracy and for a democracy. If we simplify or sanitize learning experiences, the results will be irrelevant to students' lives and to our society. Instead, we can infuse our classrooms with complexity and opportunities, knowing that the outcomes will be unpredictable and require us to engage with strategy and care.

For Teachers

It is my hope that the classroom examples, student voices, and ideas in this book breathe life into multiple paths of what it might mean to teach for a living democracy. Teaching for a living democracy is many things. It is inquiry rooted in ideas of equity. It is project-based learning with a lens of social justice. It is a community- and student-centered way of investigating and reconfiguring reality, encouraging students and teachers to inhabit the role of intellectuals and creators. It will be unique to your classroom, be different in May than it is in September, and be a continual reflection of and response to the unique aspects of your context. Most of all, it is a way to change the experience of school into humanizing acts of deep learning where students and teachers work in relationship, creating meaning on multiple levels. Our society desperately needs people equipped to struggle, create, and collaborate in visionary ways as they challenge injustice and claim power. Changing the experience of school enables youth to understand and embrace these roles, ultimately changing what it means to live.

Unlike teaching manuals that offer prescribed steps or tricks, this is a text that you, reader, must decide how to use. In the spirit of inquiry and creation, I ask:

- In what ways might you shift, expand, and humanize your pedagogy?
- What different openings for inquiry and experiences can you develop, making space for your students to reconfigure their understandings and engage with issues of the world?
- What can your students create, allowing them to generate complex ideas and reimagine their abilities?

This is not a process to be undertaken in isolation. You can begin by educating yourself on compelling content: Explore different modes of research, discover engaging scholarship or art and use it as model work and inspiration for your students. It will be helpful to turn to colleagues, experts, or networks to help you develop your ideas and get additional resources. Closely observe your students and talk to them about their learning, interests, and daily realities. Develop learning plans that provide structure while also encouraging choice and creativity alongside opportunities to create and share work.

I imagine that there are some who will read parts of this book and be quick to reject what they see as school work that maybe "lacks certain forms of rigor" or "doesn't meet clear academic standards." When one maintains a limited vision of school it is easy to develop rationales for the rejection of alternate paths. Instead, we can develop new understandings about student potential and achievement in order to change the meaning and relevancy of terms like rigor and standards. A sad truth is that many teachers face the challenge of developing their practice in the midst of unsupportive systems. It is my hope that the ideas and the student voices in this book offer support, encouraging teachers to press on, to continue to develop insights and new pedagogies, leading students toward transgressive learning experiences.

There were times, earlier in my education career, when it felt like I was approaching the end of a teaching journey. I struggled to imagine how I would sustain my teaching practice, fearing that I was steadily losing inspiration and access to a creative life. The daily reality was overflowing with challenges. I never felt as if I was able to provide enough in a system where everyone was stretched thin. Would I be able to develop a practice and a connection with students based on more than compliance?

My relationship to my teaching career changed as I learned to circumvent ideas of school that did not serve teachers or students. By rooting my practice in ideas of discovery, creativity, and dignity, my students were able to experience what it meant to produce work that nourished them rather than submitting to an outside authority or system.

I feel like it [this classroom] is a place where I can create a connection, and I am not only eating up facts that are thrown at me.
(From Haisha's final portfolio)

I began to share my practice with more and more people, finding ways to collaborate with artists and scholars who offered students inspiration and insight. The path of my own growth and transformation intertwined with the daily experiences of students in my classes. The more I was able to let go of aspects of teaching that did not serve either of us, the more they were given the opportunity to inhabit the roles of creators and agents directing aspects of their own learning. This shift challenged them to deeply examine themselves and the world while producing work that went beyond their understandings of their own abilities.

> In order to understand yourself you have to find out what you believe in and what impact you want to have on the world . . . I have thought deeply about what kind of person I want to be and how can the actions that I make have an impact on the world.
> (From Ameenah's final portfolio)

My own work, and the work of my students, has become "a means by which people discover themselves and their potential as they give names to things around them" (Shaull in foreword to Freire, 2005, p. 32–33). Teaching has changed me as a person, helping me develop compassion as young people and I spend our days together, developing new understandings. Experiences with students have deepened my knowledge of what it means to be human and the varied ways people make sense of the world they have *and* the world they want.

> There's different sides to ourselves that we don't really see at a first glance. . . . Throughout the year, I've been able to see parts of myself that I haven't seen before. Some parts surprised me and some parts led me to believe that there is something inside of me worth searching for and worth continuing beyond [the] classroom.
> (From Symone's final portfolio)

Teaching for a living democracy means committing ourselves to practices and structures that value students as people with complex human needs. It means sometimes waking up in the night preoccupied with students, feeling despair about the challenges of the work. Teaching for a living democracy is a way of fully interacting with the world, filling our days with ideas, creativity, hope, and possibility.

> Throughout the year I've learned what hope and dreams can do for a society.
> (From Jasmin's final portfolio)

Additional Classroom Resources

SECTION A: STUDENT WORK AND PROJECT EXAMPLES

- Modern-Day de Tocqueville Projects: tinyurl.com/tfald1
- Ellen's paper, *Beyond Translating:* tinyurl.com/tfald2
  Ellen's Digital Story: tinyurl.com/tfald3
- Design Your Own Learning Projects, 2016: tinyurl.com/tfald4
- Design Your Own Learning Projects, 2017: tinyurl.com/tfald5
- Design Your Own Learning: For the Love of Brown Girls: tinyurl.com/tfald6
- SLA Plays, 2016: tinyurl.com/tfald7
- The Re-PLACE-ing Project: tinyurl.com/tfald8
- Our Philadelphia, Our America: tinyurl.com/tfald9
- Art in the Open / Leah Stein Dance Company Collaboration: tinyurl.com/tfald10
- Immigration Profile: The College Educated Tofu Worker: tinyurl.com/tfald11
- Immigration Profile: Life Journey of Jose: tinyurl.com/tfald12
- Immigration Profile: Love, Culturally Divided: tinyurl.com/tfald13
- Immigration Oral History Projects (Welcoming Center): tinyurl.com/tfald14
- Education Vision Projects: tinyurl.com/tfald15
- SLA's Social Justice Alphabet: tinyurl.com/tfald16
- Inside Out Project, 2016: tinyurl.com/tfald17
- Amanda's Story: When the Bullied Becomes the Bully: tinyurl.com/tfald18
- More Student Projects Examples and Teaching Resources: mrjblock.com

SECTION B: STUDENT LESSON PLANNING TEMPLATE

Project Description and Goals:

SLA 12th-graders will be *literacy agents*, working with students in local middle schools to improve reading, writing, and thinking. SLA students will plan high-interest, participatory, literacy-based lessons and have these lessons approved by Mr. Block and the teacher who will host them. After teaching, SLA students will complete a reflection assignment.

How to design and write a lesson plan (copy these headings into your planning doc):

I.   **Choose a topic and figure out a rationale for the lesson.** (Your lesson must challenge people to reexamine assumptions, encourage people to reflect on their beliefs, or focus on compelling stories. The teachers will provide some framework but you can also look for inspiration in current events, social issues, or various texts you encounter.)

II. **What is the goal of the lesson?** (State this clearly and specifically. Example: Students will develop a deeper understanding of language, diversity of speech patterns, and discrimination that occurs based on how people speak.)

III. **What is the opening?** (A quote for a journal? A picture with questions for discussion? A poem for analysis?) This part of the lesson should get everyone thinking in preparation for what comes later.

IV. **Introduce the content in an engaging way.** (An article, a film, statistics for analysis . . .)

V.   **Use a method for analysis and development of ideas.** (Discussion questions, figure out something with a group . . .)

VI. **Closing/Final Thoughts** (How will you wrap up the lesson?)

SECTION C: SAMPLE SELF-EVALUATION/PEER REVIEW FORMS

Example 1: Modern-Day de Tocqueville Project

Modern-Day de Tocqueville Self-Evaluation

Title of your chapter: _____

Deep question you are investigating:

Main argument of your chapter:

In your opinion, what are the strongest parts of your chapter? Why?

In your opinion, what are the parts of your chapter that fall short? Why, and what is your plan to improve these parts?

Modern-Day de Tocqueville Peer Review

Name of Reviewer _____

Four Things That Are Working Well in the Chapter:

Three Specific Ideas for Improvement:

Two Questions to Ask the Author for Clarity:

One Source That You Recommend for the Author:

Example 2: Our Philadelphia, Our America

Field Note Self-Evaluation

1. How does your Field Note connect to the larger goals of this project? What will make it interesting or important for readers?

2. In what ways does your Field Note help readers understand your topic as if they are there, experiencing it? How can this descriptive aspect of your writing be improved?

3. What larger ideas or issues are raised by your Field Note? How can this aspect be further developed?

Field Note Peer Review

Reviewed by: _____
1. What are the strengths of the draft of the Field Note? (List at least three.)

2. What questions do you have for the author to help them revise and improve this Field Note? (List at least three.)

3. Field Notes cannot be published until they are polished and presentable to a wider audience. What specific grammar and writing revisions does this author need to make in order to publish?

SECTION D: DESIGN YOUR OWN
LEARNING PROJECT REQUIREMENTS

Design Your Own Learning

The final part of our course will be devoted to Design Your Own Learning projects. These projects offer you an opportunity to choose a topic you find compelling and then research, create, and present your work to a wider audience. One way to think of this project is to focus on **untold stories** or **hidden realities.**

All projects must have the following components:

- A compelling question for investigation
- Reading list and research plan
- An official proposal, pitch, and approval

- Production and creation, including multiple drafts and feedback
- Final product that includes writing (minimum 500 words) and media
- A process of sharing your work with targeted audiences

Potential Project Ideas

- What different realities exist on a block? In a neighborhood? In a city?
- How is _____ neighborhood changing?
- What are the stories of minimum-wage workers?
- What does it mean to be a refugee?
- What do people fear? What do they value?
- What can we learn from the stories of police officers?
- How do people organize and change their reality?
- What are the untold stories of a neighborhood?
- Or (maybe the best option) Come up with another idea!
- Student Work Models: (See online document: tinyurl.com/tfald26)

Your Proposal Must Include

I.   Question for investigation and goal of your project.
II. Research: How will you learn about your topic? What different models do you have for your work? (Must include at least four annotated sources.)
III. Process: How will you go about creating your product?
IV. What is the final product? Who will see it? How will it influence people?

SECTION E: ADVANCED ESSAY GUIDELINES

Essential Questions:

- How do violence and war change people?
- In what different ways is militarism ingrained in our society?
- Can we imagine a society rooted in nonviolence?

Advanced Essay: 750–1,000 words on the themes of Violence, Militarism, and/or Alternatives. Must include:

- Outside evidence and description of an image
- Detailed analysis of sources and issues
- Development of complex larger idea (a.k.a. argument or thesis)
- Resource Bank: (available in online document) tinyurl.com/tfald20

SECTION F: ADVANCED ESSAY RUBRIC

Design	Paper engages readers in a complex issue. From the beginning writing is descriptive, detailed, and insightful.
Knowledge	Paper uses relevant sources in the form of outside texts, description of an image, and/or scenes of memory.
Application	Essay smoothly moves between evidence, analysis, and development of larger idea and insights.
Presentation	Precise control of language, stylistic techniques, and sentence structures that create a consistent and effective tone.
Process	Steps are completed on time. There is evidence of quality peer reviews and detailed revision.

SECTION G: MEDIA COVERAGE OF STUDENT WORK

- The Benefits and Challenges of Student-Designed Learning: tinyurl.com/tfald21
  When Black Teens Get Real About America's Love of Light Skin: tinyurl.com/tfald22
  Philadelphia Students Become Modern-Day de Tocquevilles: tinyurl.com/tfald23
- How Inquiry Can Enable Students to be Modern-Day de Tocquevilles: tinyurl.com/tfald24
  Philadelphia Art Installation Examines the Nexus of Language, Power, and Culture: tinyurl.com/tfald25

SECTION H: RECOMMENDED OUTSIDE RESOURCES—ORGANIZATIONS AND NETWORKS

Clear the Air—A group of educators who believe "community, learning and dialogue are essential to our personal and professional development, [that] we have the power and responsibility to lay the foundations necessary to create a more just and equitable society, [and that] education is a vehicle for social change." (cleartheaireducation.wordpress.com)

Disrupt Texts—"A crowdsourced, grassroots effort by teachers for teachers to challenge the traditional canon in order to create a more inclusive, representative, and equitable language arts curriculum that our students deserve. It is part of our mission to aid and develop teachers committed to anti-racist/anti-bias teaching pedagogy and practices." (disrupttexts.org)

Education for Liberation—"A national coalition of teachers, community activists, researchers, youth, and parents who believe education should teach people . . . how to understand and challenge the injustices their communities face." (edliberation.org)

Educolor— "Seeks to elevate the voices of public school advocates of color on educational equity and justice. We are an inclusive cooperative of informed, inspired, and motivated educators, parents, students, writers, and activists who promote and embrace the centrality of substantive intersectional diversity." (educolor.org)

Edutopia—Dedicated to "transforming K–12 education so that all students can acquire and effectively apply the knowledge, attitudes, and skills necessary to thrive in their studies, careers, and adult lives." (edutopia.org)

Facing History and Ourselves—"Helps students connect choices made in the past to those they will confront in their own lives. . . . Resources address racism, antisemitism, and prejudice at pivotal moments in history." (facinghistory.org)

Marginal Syllabus—"Convenes and sustains conversations with educators about issues of equity in teaching, learning, and education. . . . Collaborates with authors whose writing may be considered contrary—or marginal—to dominant education and schooling norms." (marginalsyllab.us)

National Writing Project—"Focuses the knowledge, expertise, and leadership of our nation's educators on sustained efforts to improve writing and learning for all learners." (nwp.org)

Progressive Education Network—"Believes that the purpose of education transcends preparation for college or career. Schools nurture citizens in an increasingly diverse democracy. . . . Promotes a vision of progressive education for the 21st century." (progressiveeducationnetwork.org)

Rethinking Schools—An activist publication with articles written for and by teachers, parents, and students. Also publishers of a range of books for educators. (rethinkingschools.org)

Teaching for Change—"Provides teachers and parents with the tools to create schools where students learn to read, write, and change the world." (teachingforchange.org)

Teaching Tolerance—Aims to "to help teachers and schools educate children and youth to be active participants in a diverse democracy." Provide free resources to educators with "an emphasis on social justice and anti-bias" education. (tolerance.org)

The Zinn Education Project—"Promotes and supports the teaching of people's history in classrooms across the country." (www.zinnedproject.org)

References

Adichie, C. N. (2009, July). The danger of a single story. *TEDGlobal.* Retrieved from www.ted.com/talks/chimamanda_adichie_the_danger_of_a_single_story?language=en.

Alexander, M. (2004, November 26). Telling my son about Ferguson. *New York Times.* Retrieved from www.nytimes.com/2014/11/26/opinion/ferguson-telling-my-son-michelle-alexander.html

Anzaldúa, G. (2007). *Borderlands: La frontera.* San Francisco, CA: Aunt Lute Books.

Arendt, H. (2018). *The human condition* (2nd ed). Chicago, IL: University of Chicago Press.

Auer, P. (Ed.). (2013). *Code-switching in conversation: Language, interaction, and identity.* New York, NY: Routledge.

Baldwin, A., Hercules, B., & Orenstein, B. (1999). *The democratic promise: Saul Alinsky & his legacy* [Film]. Berkeley, CA: University of California Extension Center for Media and Independent Learning.

Baldwin, J. (1979, July 29). If Black English isn't a language, then tell me, what is? *New York Times.* Retrieved from archive.nytimes.com/www.nytimes.com/books/98/03/29/specials/baldwin-english.html?source=post_page

Block, J. (2016). Inter-Composition No. 2. In D. F. Burchfield & L. Bakst (Eds), *Primary Sources: Materials for a New Cultural Archive* (pp. 30–32). Philadelphia, PA: Re-PLACE-ing Philadelphia.

Boggs, G. L., & Kurashige, S. (2012). *The next American revolution: Sustainable activism for the twenty-first century.* Berkeley, CA: University of California Press.

Campbell, J., & Moyers, B. D. (1988). *The power of myth.* New York, NY: Doubleday.

Coalition of Essential Schools Common Principles. (n.d.). Retrieved from essentialschools.org/common-principles/

Coates, T. (2017). *Between the world and me.* New York, NY: Random House.

Cochran-Smith, M., & Lytle, S. L. (2009). *Inquiry as stance: Practitioner research for the next generation.* New York, NY: Teachers College Press.

Cook-Sather, A. (2009). *Learning from the student's perspective: A sourcebook for effective teaching.* Boulder, CO: Paradigm.

Dewey, J. (1897). My pedagogic creed. *School Journal, 54,* 77–80

Dewey, J. (1933) *How we think.* New York, NY: D. C. Heath.

Dewey, J. (1967). *The early works, 1882–1898.* J. A. Boydston (Ed.). Carbondale, IL: Southern Illinois University Press.

DiYanni, R., & Hoy, P. C. (2008). *Occasions for writing: Evidence, idea, essay.* Boston, MA: Thomson Heinle.

Douglass, F. (1857). Two Speeches. Retrieved from archive.org/stream/ASPC0001937700/ASPC0001937700_djvu.txt

Dwyer, L. (2016, February 11). When Black teens get real about America's love of light skin. *TakePart.* Retrieved from www.takepart.com/article/2016/02/11/when-black-teens-get-real-about-americas-love-light-skin

Elbow, P. (2007). *Writing without teachers.* New York, NY: Oxford University Press.

Elliott, A. (2013, December 9). Invisible child. *New York Times.* Retrieved from www.nytimes.com/projects/2013/invisible-child/index.html

Elliott, S. (2015). *Teaching and learning on the verge: Democratic education in action.* New York, NY: Teachers College Press.

Freire, P. (1983). The importance of the act of reading. *Journal of Education 165*(1), 5–11. Retrieved from journals.sagepub.com/doi/abs/10.1177/002205748316500103

Freire, P. (2005). *Pedagogy of the oppressed.* New York, NY: Continuum.

Giroux, H. A. (2005). *Border crossings: Cultural workers and the politics of education.* New York, NY: Routledge.

Goffman, A. (2015). *On the run: Fugitive life in an American city.* New York, NY: Picador/Farrar, Straus and Giroux.

Greene, M. (2000). *Releasing the imagination: Essays on education, the arts, and social change.* San Francisco, CA: Jossey-Bass.

Guinier, L., & Torres, G. (2015, June 29). The miner's canary. *The Nation.* Retrieved from www.thenation.com/article/miners-canary/

Hagopian, J. (2015). *More than a score: The new uprising against high-stakes testing.* Chicago, IL: Haymarket Books.

Hamid, M. (2017). *Exit west.* Haryana, India: Penguin Random House.

Harris, V. J. (2007). In praise of a scholarly force: Rudine Sims Bishop. *Language Arts, 85*(2), 153–159. Retrieved from library.ncte.org/journals/la/issues/v85-2

hooks, b. (2017). *Teaching to transgress: Education as the practice of freedom.* New York, NY: Routledge.

Hurston, Z. N. (2006). *Their eyes were watching God.* New York, NY: Harper Perennial Modern Classics.

Illich, I. (1983). *Deschooling society.* New York, NY: Harper Colophon.

Kay, M. R. (2018). *Not light, but fire: How to lead meaningful race conversations in the classroom.* Portsmouth, NH: Stenhouse Publishers.

King, Center. (2019, January 8). The King Philosophy. Retrieved from thekingcenter.org/king-philosophy/#sub4

Kozol, J. (2005). *The shame of the nation: The restoration of apartheid schooling in America.* New York, NY: Crown Publishers.

Ladson-Billings, G. (2009). *The dreamkeepers: Successful teachers of African American children.* San Francisco, CA: Jossey-Bass.

Lakey, G. (2010). *Facilitating group learning strategies for success with diverse adult learners.* San Francisco, CA: Jossey-Bass.

Lakey, G. (2013, February 22). Re-writing an attacker's script—getting in practice. *Waging Nonviolence.* Retrieved from wagingnonviolence.org/2013/09/re-writing-attackers-script/

Larsen, N. (1997). *Passing*. New York, NY: Penguin Books. (Original work published in 1929.)

Lehmann, C., & Chase, Z. (2015). *Building school 2.0: How to create the schools we need*. San Francisco, CA: Jossey-Bass.

Lorde, A. (1998). *Sister outsider*. Freedom, CA: Crossing Press.

McIntosh, P. (2003). White privilege: Unpacking the invisible knapsack. In S. Plous (Ed.), *Understanding prejudice and discrimination* (pp. 191–196). New York, NY: McGraw-Hill.

McTighe, J., & Wiggins, G. P. (2013). *Essential questions: Opening doors to student understanding*. Alexandria, VA: ASCD.

Meier, D. (2005). *The power of their ideas: Lessons for America from a small school in Harlem*. Boston, MA: Beacon Press.

Milne, A. (2017). *Coloring in the white spaces: Reclaiming cultural identity in whitestream schools*. New York: Peter Lang.

Milne, A. (2019, March 25). White supremacy in our classrooms. *Education Central*. Retrieved from educationcentral.co.nz/opinion-ann-milne-white-supremacy-in-our-classrooms/

Mindell, A. (2014). *Sitting in the fire: Large group transformation using conflict and diversity*. Florence, OR, & San Francisco, CA.: Deep Democracy Exchange.

Morreira, S., & Luckett, K. (2019, July 01). Questions academics can ask to decolonise their classrooms. Retrieved from theconversation.com/questions-academics-can-ask-to-decolonise-their-classrooms-103251

Morrison, T. (2013, March). Interview with Claudia Brodsky, Cornell University. [Video]. Retrieved from www.youtube.com/watch?reload=9&v=FAs3E1AgNeM

New Zealand Ministry of Education. (2013). *Kahikitia, Accelerating success*. Retrieved from education.govt.nz/assets/Documents/Ministry/Strategies-and-policies/Ka-Hikitia/KaHikitiaAcceleratingSuccessEnglish.pdf.

Noddings, N. (2002). *Educating moral people: A caring alternative to character education*. New York, NY: Teachers College Press.

O'Brien, Tim. (1998) *The things they carried*. New York, NY: Broadway Books.

Paris, D., & Alim, H. S. (2017). *Culturally sustaining pedagogies: Teaching and learning for justice in a changing world*. New York, NY: Teachers College Press.

Paris, D., Alim, H. S., & Ferlazzo, L. (2017, July 6). Author Interview: "Culturally Sustaining Pedagogies." *Education Week*. Retrieved from blogs.edweek.org/teachers/classroom_qa_with_larry_ferlazzo/2017/07/author_interview_culturally_sustaining_pedagogies.html

Phunthavong, V. (2015, April 19). Crossing to Saftey. *New York Times*. Retrieved from www.nytimes.com/2015/04/19/magazine/crossing-to-safety.html

Piercy, M. (2002). *Circles on the water: selected poems of Marge Piercy*. New York, NY: Knopf.

Rankine, C. (2015). *Citizen: An American lyric*. London, UK: Penguin Books.

Rankine, C. (2019, July 17). I wanted to know what White men thought about their privilege. So I asked. *The New York Times Magazine*. Retrieved from https://www.nytimes.com/2019/07/17/magazine/white-men-privilege.html

Ravitch, Diane. (2011). *The death and life of the great American school system: how testing and choice are undermining education*. New York, NY: Basic Books,

Re-PLACE-ing Philadelphia. (n.d.). Retrieved from rc-place-ing.org/about-us/re-place-ing-philadelphia

Rose, M. (2005). *Lives on the boundary: A moving account of the struggles and achievements of Americas educationally unprepared.* New York, NY: Penguin Books.

Rose, M. (2009). *Why school?* New York, NY: New Press.

Schwartz, K. (2015, February 10). How inquiry can enable students to become modern day de Tocquevilles. MindShift. Retrieved from www.kqed.org/mindshift/39262/how-inquiry-can-enable-students-to-become-modern-day-de-tocquevilles.

Shalaby, C. (2017). *Troublemakers: Lessons in freedom from young children at school.* New York, NY: The New Press.

Sidahmed, M. (2016, November 11). "She was making her stand": Image of Baton Rouge protester an instant classic. *The Guardian.* Retrieved from www.theguardian.com/us-news/2016/jul/11/baton-rouge-protester-photo-iesha-evans

Sims Bishop, R. (1990). Mirrors, windows, and sliding glass doors. *Perspectives, 1*(3), ix–xi.

Solnit, R. (2016). *Hope in the dark: Untold history of people power.* Chicago, IL: Haymarket Books.

Spirit in Action. (2010). *Guide to Working in Diverse Groups.* Retrieved from spiritinaction.net/wpsia/wp-content/uploads/2018/06/Guide-to-Working-in-Diverse-Groups-Web-Version-Single-Pages.pdf

Three New York International High Schools. (2006). *Forty-cent tip: Stories of New York City immigrant workers.* Providence, RI: Next Generation Press.

Tomlins-Jahnke, H., & Durie, A. (2008). *Whanau socialisation through everyday talk: A pilot study.* Wellington, NZ: Families Commission.

Training for Change. (2018). Mainstream & Margin. Retrieved from https://www.trainingforchange.org/training_tools/mainstream-margin/

Turkle, S. (2012, April 21). The flight from conversation. *New York Times.* Retrieved from www.nytimes.com/2012/04/22/opinion/sunday/the-flight-from-conversation.html?_r=1

Tyack, D., & Cuban, L. (1995). *Tinkering toward utopia a century of public school reform.* Cambridge, MA: Harvard University Press.

Vargas, J. A. (Director). (2013). *Documented* [Video file]. Retrieved from documentedthefilm.com/

Whitman, W. (2005*). Walt Whitman's Leaves of grass: The first (1855) edition.* New York, NY: Penguin Books.

Wiggins, G. P., & McTighe, J. (2005). *Understanding by design* (2nd ed.). Alexandria, VA: Association for Supervision and Curriculum Development.

Zinn, H. (2002). *The power of nonviolence: Writings by advocates of peace.* Boston, MA: Beacon Press.

Index

About the Author

Joshua Block teaches public high school students English and history in Philadelphia. He is a teacher educator, national board certified teacher, and recipient of a Fulbright Distinguished Award in Teaching.